Mel Bay's SCHOOL OF

Banjo
Bluegrass "Melodic" Style

GW00729014

Unlock the mysteries for playing and working out songs in this popular 3-Finger Melodic Style. Features 30 step-by-step lessons and 24 popular fiddle and bluegrass tunes!
* This picking style is often referred to as Keith Style, Fiddle Style, & Melodic Style.

Each lesson is demonstrated with a tune which can also be learned independently of the lesson. In tablature and musical notation! Also includes reviews and exercises.

Substitute licks are included with the tunes for improvising and working out your own arrangements.

For Upper Level Beginning Players through the Advanced Level.

CD contents

1 2 3 4 5 6 7 8 9 0

Visit us on the Web at www.melbay.com — E-mail us at email@melbay.com

Table of Contents
By Lesson with Topic and Song

Alphabetical Song Index on page 4 —— Complete CD Track Index on pages 93 & 94

Table of Contents
By Lesson with Topic and Song

Alphabetical Song Index on page 4 —— Complete CD Track Index on pages 93 & 94

NOTE: Each Lesson is demonstrated with a song. The songs also include Substitute Licks. Each song can stand alone, and may be learned without reading the lesson, if so desired. The beginning of each lesson is intended especially for beginners to the melodic style. Moving down the page, the lesson becomes more advanced.

Alphabetical Song Index

Table of Contents by Lesson Index on page 2 —— Complete CD Track Index on pages 93 & 94

NOTE: Each Lesson is demonstrated with a song. The songs also include Substitute Licks. Each song can stand alone, and may be learned without reading the lesson, if so desired. The beginning of each lesson is intended especially for beginners to the melodic style. Moving down the page, the lesson becomes more advanced.

Foreword

Melodic Style Bluegrass- It's Fun!

As the Introduction will explain in more depth, the *Melodic Style* is a beautiful 3-finger picking style which can be traced to the early 1900s and became a fully accepted style for playing the 5-string banjo in the 1960s, and is today an integral part of the 3-finger style of many banjo players at all playing levels. Plus, the songs arranged in this style are easy and fun to learn. Although the melodic style may sound impossible with all of those notes coming from it, surprisingly, you will find that it is not that difficult to learn and no previous musical knowledge is needed.

This course covers the Melodic Style from the very basics of this picking style to the advanced techniques and provides many fun to play and well-known songs arranged in the 3-finger Melodic Style for upper level beginning players through advanced level players.

Recommendations on How To Use This Book:

This book can be used in many different ways, depending upon your level of playing and your objectives. Some players may simply want to learn to play the arrangements for the songs without the instruction. A beginner might learn only the main technique at the top of each lesson before learning the song. A more experienced player may want to read through each entire lesson and learn every song, in order to gain an understanding of the building processes which lead into the more advanced techniques presented later on in the course. Likewise, this course may be studied from start to finish with the objective of developing the ability to improvise and/or work out arrangements in the melodic style, as well as utilize these techniques in combination with other 3-finger styles. Jazz tunes, fiddle tunes, bluegrass tunes, and tunes belonging to virtually any type of music are beautiful when played in this style.

Above all, it is important to have fun when learning each song. If you like a particular technique and want to work with it further, look for references in that lesson to other songs which appear later in the book, yet can be played as further study for that technique as well. i.e. *Cripple Creek, Katy Hill* and *Sally Goodin'* are related to Lesson 1 even though they appear in different sections. The lessons are in step-by-step order and each lesson is demonstrated with a song. *However,* the songs are not necessarily placed in the order of difficulty. An easier song may be presented later in the course to demonstrate a new technique.

This method has worked well with my banjo students at each level. I hope it will work for you also.

Happy Pickin'!
Janet Davis

NOTE: This book is recommended for the player who has learned at least a few songs on the banjo and understands the basic left-hand hammers, slides, etc. It is written and arranged primarily for the upper level beginner through the advanced level player.

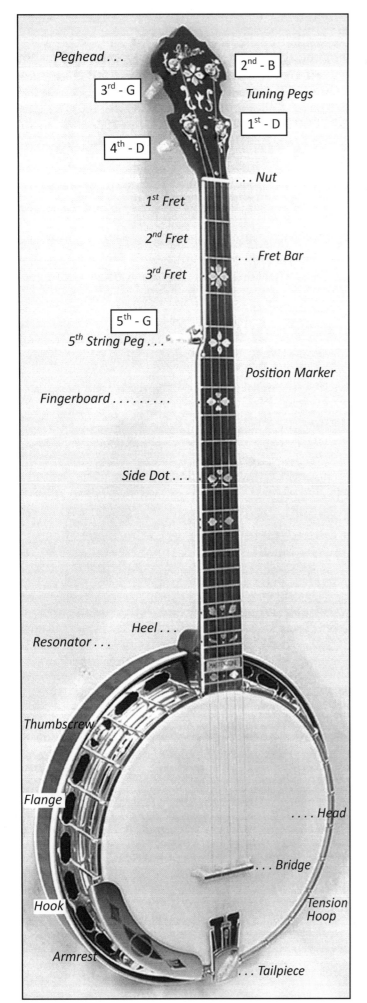

Peghead . . .

3rd - G

2nd - B

Tuning Pegs

1st - D

4th - D

. . . Nut

1st Fret

2nd Fret

. . . Fret Bar

3rd Fret

5th - G

5th String Peg . . .

Position Marker

Fingerboard . . . .

Side Dot . . .

Heel . . .

Resonator . . .

Thumbscrew

Flange

. . . . Head

. . . Bridge

Hook

Tension Hoop

Armrest

. . . Tailpiece

The Banjo & Tuning

 TRACK 2

G TUNING This is the most common tuning used for 3-finger picking. It is important to maintain the tuning of your banjo for several reasons. First, your banjo will sound better. Also, your ear will begin to develop the more you play, so that eventually, you will be able to identify chord names and note locations by ear, as well as from tab or musical notation.

An electronic "auto-tuner" is recommended as an excellent aid for tuning your banjo. This tool automatically tells you when each string is in tune and is easy to use, inexpensive.

G TUNING: **G   D   G   B   D**   (Note Names)
5th 4th 3rd 2nd 1st   (Strings)

The banjo can be tuned to itself as follows:

The strings are numbered in order: The 5th string is the short string; the 1st string is closest to the floor.

1.) Start with the 4th String – this is the deepest tone on your banjo & is normally tuned to a D (below middle C on the piano). All other strings will be tuned relative to this string.
2.) Depress the 4th string at the 5th fret to tune the open 3rd string to this pitch (G). The open 3rd string sounds like the 4th string fretted at the 5th fret.
3.) Depress the 3rd string at the 4th fret and tune the 2nd string to this pitch (B). The open 2nd string sounds like the 3rd string at the 4th fret.
4.) Press the 2nd string on the 3rd fret and tune the open 1st string to this pitch (D). The open 1st string sounds like the 2nd string fretted on the 3rd fret. (D next to middle C on the piano.)
5.) Press the 1st string at the 5th fret and tune the 5th string to this pitch. G above middle C. The open 5th string (short string) sounds like the 1st string, 5th fret.

When tuned correctly, the strings will sound a G chord when strummed. Also, the 1st and 4th strings will sound in unison an octave apart, (D notes). The 3rd and 5th strings open sound alike, an octave apart (G notes).

6

Tablature

The music in this book is written in tablature on the top staff with the optional musical notation on the bottom staff.

 TRACK 3

The melodic style is played in the traditional 3-finger style using one plastic thumb pick and two metal finger picks. The tablature format used in this book is fairly standard, and should be easy for anyone to use.

Tablature is a simple system designed for those who do not read music. It can be learned in a few minutes. Tablature appears on the staff above the musical notation in this book. It is useful even for those who read music, as it tells you where each note is played on the fingerboard.
Note: Lay the banjo flat in your lap, or lay it on a table to compare the strings in the tab with the diagram below.

1.) **The five lines are the five strings of your banjo.** Each line represents a certain string.
2.) **The numbers are fret numbers.**
Each number tells you which fret number to hold down with the left hand on that particular string (line).

For Example: 2 on the top line tells you to fret (hold down) the 2nd fret on the 1st string (closest to the floor.)
3 on the middle line means to fret the 3rd fret on the 3rd string.
0 means to pick the string open (without fretting it.)

```
1st  ——————2——————————0——————————0——————
2nd  —————————————————————————————————————
3rd  —————0——————————0——————————3——————————
4th  —————————————————————————————————————
5th  ———————————————0——————————0——————————
```

SUMMARY:
The lines tell you which string to pick.
The numbers tell you which fret number to hold, (on that string), with the left hand.
(Two numbers, one over the other, are to be played at the same time, unless indicated otherwise. This is called a pinch.)
Note: Push the string down between the metal fret bars, not on the metal bar.

RIGHT HAND FINGERS: T = Thumb; I = Index; M = Middle
Only three fingers pick the strings with the right hand. (These are indicated below the notes in the tablature).

LEFT HAND FINGERS: t = thumb; i = index; m = middle; r = ring; p = pinky
Left-hand fingering appears *above* the notes (numbers in the tablature) in difficult areas.

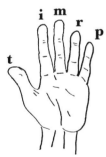

Fretting Fingers
(Left hand)

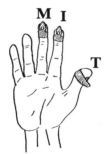

Picking Fingers
(Right hand)

Fretboard Over Staff = L.H. fingering "Shape"
(not a chord)

ROLL PATTERNS for the Right Hand: Each "roll" pattern is a right-hand fingering pattern or picking sequence. Hold any chord or set of notes with the left hand (open = G chord). In the melodic style, the left hand usually holds a scale shape when a roll pattern is played with the right hand. A song may use a roll for every measure with the right hand, as you will see in *Cripple Creek,* or by mixing the roll patterns as in *Blackberry Blossom.* However, the melodic style does not adhere strictly to playing the roll patterns as it also works with melodic scale patterns. Note: Each roll can begin with any string; it is simply a right-hand fingering sequence which often occurs in songs played on the 5-string banjo.
There are five basic roll patterns: Each "roll" consists of 8 eighth notes = 1 measure of music.

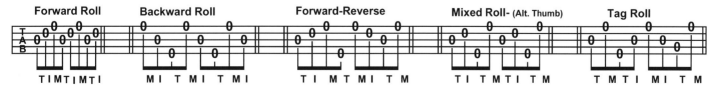

Rhythm

Good timing is very important when playing the banjo.

Stems:
The *duration,* or length of time each note should *ring* is indicated by the *stem,* or line which is drawn from each number or note. This is referred to as the rhythm or timing.

Note: The stems for the rhythm in tablature are exactly the same as the stems used for the musical notation.

The basic unit in banjo music is called an "eighth" note

There will be 8 eighth notes in one measure of tablature.
Each eighth note should receive *equal* duration.
Do not hold one note longer than another.

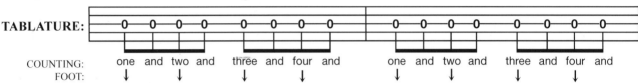

The eighth notes should be picked evenly through both measures, without stopping between the measures.
The listener should not know there are divisions in your tablature.
The bar lines make it easier to learn to play the song correctly. The stems tell you how long to let each note ring.
(Single eighth notes have a flag. Two or four eighth notes are connected with a single "beam".)

The next most common unit is a "quarter" note.

The quarter note is held (should ring) twice as long as an eighth note.
Hold the quarter note for the duration of 2 eighth notes.

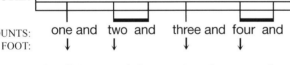

The "sixteenth" note is often used with slides, hammers & pull offs.

Play two sixteenth notes for the duration of one eighth note.
Play four sixteenth notes for the duration of one quarter note. Sixteenth notes are connected by a double beam.

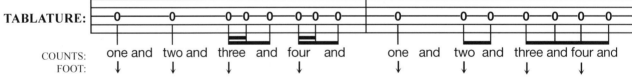

All of the stems (rhythm) in this book for the tab and music follow the musical notation standards in 4/4 time unless noted.

RESTS:
This indicates silence for the same duration.
Do not play for the equivalent number of beats indicated by the rest.

Syncopation: commonly used in the melodic style.   Short - Long
Hold the quarter note for the duration of 2 eighth notes.

Triplets: three notes are played in the same amount of time as 2 eighth notes are normally played.
This will be explained in the Lesson where triplets are presented. Triplets are often used in the Melodic Style.

Additional Symbols & Guidelines

Standard tablature indications for hammers, pull offs, rhythmic indications, etc. are used throughout this book when these left-hand techniques occur. (See "Tablature Explanations" for left & right-hand fingering indications.)

LEFT-HAND TECHNIQUES: H, P, SL, CH = are techniques used by the left hand to sound the strings with the left hand without picking them with the right hand. The right hand picks the preceding note. (Often the right hand will simultaneously pick a different note at the same time the left hand sounds the note.)

H = **Hammer** the fret indicated by pushing down the string with the left finger hard enough to sound the tone.

P = **Pull off** (or push off) the string from the fret before the note to be sounded by the pull off to sound the note.

SL = **Slide** to the fret number above the SL with the left finger from the number before it.

Ch↑ = **Bend** (choke) the string with the left finger, after picking the note to raise the tone.

Ch↓ = **Bend** the string with the left finger before picking the note, then straighten it to lower the pitch.

ADDITONAL Markings:

> = **Accent:** Emphasize the note –i.e. play it louder.

( ) = **Implied or Optional Note,** it surrounds a note. Sustain the previous note if you do not play this note.

( ) = **Implied or Optional Chord.** A chord in parenthesis may be substituted for the standard chord indicated.

= **Tie:** Two identical notes are "tied" together. Only the first note is played. Sustain this tone through the second note; do not pick the second note.

= **L.H. Shape:** Hold the two notes with the left hand before picking the notes one at a time with the right hand.

||: :|| = **Repeat Sign:** play again before continuing. Return to the previous repeat sign with dots facing it, if there is one; Otherwise, return to the beginning of the song and repeat the section. The measure numbers also indicate the repeats.

⌐1.⌐ ⌐2.⌐ = **Endings 1 and 2:** Play through Ending 1 to the repeat sign; repeat the section; substitute Ending 2 the second time.

MEASURE NUMBERS & Substitute Licks:

The measures in each song are numbered in the order in which they should be played.
This will help you follow the repeated sections AND the alternate licks at the end of each song can be substituted in the song for the indicated measure number(s), to make the song easier and/or more difficult, more fun to play, or to create a second variation.

FORM – Sections or Parts: A B C D

Songs are divided into sections, which make up the "form." For example, "Verse" & "Chorus," if the song has words, or with letters, as "Part A," "Part B," etc. when they are instrumentals. When learning a new song, it is easiest to learn it one section at a time. Also, it is important to notice if a Part is to be repeated before you continue with the next section. These sections will be indicated in the arrangement. Fiddle tunes, which are so often played in the melodic style, are usually built with Part A played twice, followed by Part B repeated.

PICK UP NOTES: Many arrangements begin with a partial measure labeled "pick-up notes."
This measure is only intended to begin the song. If coming in with a band, in the middle of the performance, this measure should be played with the last measure of the arrangement played just before it.

A Brief History *of the Melodic Style*

The traditional "Bluegrass" 3-finger picking style (Scruggs style) was introduced and popularized by Earl Scruggs, who played banjo with Bill Monroe and His Bluegrass Boys in the early 1940s. Another 3-finger picking style, based upon emulating the fiddle on the banjo, followed in its footsteps as an accepted picking style in the early 1960s, when it was introduced and popularized by Bill Keith. He, too, was playing banjo with Bill Monroe and His Bluegrass Boys (1963) when the world first became fascinated with this new sound from the 5-string banjo. This style has been referred to as "fiddle style," "melodic style," "chromatic style," "Keith style," and a multitude of other names. However, today, *Melodic Style* is generally the accepted name, as almost every note played is a melody note.

Melodic Style picking actually dates back to the early 1900s, during the classical era on the 5-string banjo. However, it was not recognized as its own definitive style of 3-finger picking for the banjo until the early 1960s. In 1961, Bill Keith won a major banjo contest playing *Devil's Dream* and *Sailor's Hornpipe* in his new style. By 1963, when banjo players and audiences all over the country heard Bill Keith playing with Bill Monroe on tours and especially on the Grand Ole Opry, the "new" *Melodic Style,* became a reality in the world of bluegrass banjo. About the same time, another banjo player, Bobby Thompson, who played with Carl Story and Jim & Jesse in the late 1950s and mid 1960s, independently came up with similar ideas, playing the banjo note for note along with the fiddle. By the time Bobby was playing his now infamous melodic banjo run for the popular TV series, *Hee Haw* to open and close each show, the public wanted to hear more and banjo players everywhere were trying to figure out how to play like this.

In the 1970s, the melodic style was a live topic among banjo players and even became quite controversial. There were traditional Scruggs Style players, who were avidly against this style, while others were thrilled with the innovative new style of playing. I have privately wondered if some of those players who were against playing in this style, simply did not have the understanding of how to play in this style. Audiences certainly seemed to enjoy both the traditional and the newer sounds.

Although the Melodic Style began its popularity with fiddle tunes, banjo players began adding more blues notes, and chromatic tones. *Newgrass* became a popular term for the people who were the progressive players of the time. "Do you play Bluegrass or Newgrass?" was a common question at festivals and in jam sessions in the late 1970s and through the 1980s. *Newgrass* eventually developed into a full blown "Chromatic Style" using the chromatic scale. And, banjo players have continued to experiment.

The traditional "bluegrass" 3-finger style which began in the 1940s when Earl Scruggs played with Bill Monroe and His Bluegrass Boys, met a fork in the road in the 1960s when Bill Keith introduced and popularized the new "fiddle style" or "melodic" style. Some players remained true to the traditional 1940s bluegrass rolls and licks in a very chordal fashion and continued to develop within this realm, while another avenue opened up for the development of 3-finger picking working with scale lines. New 5-string banjo players have been raised on the now accepted developments from the 1960s forward.

Today, in the 21st century, the true "melodic style" as presented in the book, is the foundation of the more progressive styles and is today a very popular and effective way to play the banjo throughout an entire song, especially for fiddle tunes. The Melodic Style is also often blended with and combined with other 3-finger sounds, including the traditional bluegrass Scruggs Style. The above will be demonstrated as you travel through the lessons and songs in this book.

NOTE: To hear a few of the outstanding professional banjo players who have adapted and contributed to the development of the Melodic Style in their own right, listen to recordings by Bill Keith, Bobby Thompson, Carl Jackson, Alan Munde, Garland Shuping, Larry McNeely, Courtney Johnson, Tony Trischka, Bela Fleck, Scott Vestal, and Carroll Best (1932 – 1995 who told me he had played his banjo in this style all his life, and had learned it from his Mama, who had played it all her life.)

Introduction: What Is Melodic Style?

When the melodic style first became a 'valid' and accepted way to play the banjo in the 1960s, no one knew exactly what to call it. This style has been called "fiddle style," "melodic style," "chromatic style," "Keith style," and a multitude of different names. However, today, *Melodic Style* is generally the accepted name as almost every note played is a melody note. This style is not difficult to play. The key is simply to understand the basics involved in this 3-finger style of picking.

Songs played on the banjo in the *Melodic Style* involve playing the same notes that a fiddle player might use for these songs. The right-hand fingers pick the strings in the same manner used to play the traditional bluegrass or Scruggs style. Instead of holding chord positions with the left hand however, the left-hand fingers will normally hold scale positions *in pairs,* fretting two notes at a time. This is fairly simple as only three left-hand scale positions are used in the basic major scale for many songs. These will be presented one at a time in the instructional lessons. The same left-hand positions are used in many different songs and they are easy to learn.

Traditional bluegrass roll patterns are played by the right hand in the Melodic Style. However, different fingering patterns are also required in order to include all of the melody notes. In the Melodic Style, the 5th string is often a melody note, rather than a drone string. Every note played in the melodic style is either a melody note or a passing tone which connects the melody notes. Of course, there will always be exceptions.

Because the Key of G is so natural to the 5-string banjo and most banjo players are comfortable playing in this key, it should be very easy to understand how the melody for each song is drawn from this scale line. Much of this book will be based around songs which are played in the Key of G, although other scales (i.e. modal, pentatonic) and keys will also be covered in this course. Remember, this will be easy to understand if you follow the lessons in order. By the end of this course you should know Melodic Style arrangements for many popular bluegrass and fiddle tunes as well as understand how to work out your own arrangements in this style.

Summary

Melodic Style picking can be and is used to play just about any type of song on the banjo and fiddle tunes are especially beautiful when played by the banjo in this style. The banjo emulates the fiddle in the Melodic Style by working along the major scale line to play the melody notes, as well as the fill in notes, rather than working primarily from chord positions, as it does when playing in Scruggs style. Fiddle tunes often have so many melody notes that it is difficult to incorporate all of the notes with the Scruggs style rolls and licks. The Melodic Style enables the banjo player to include all of the melody notes as well as to smoothly span the entire fingerboard to accommodate a tune with a wide tonal range.

This 3-finger banjo style can be enjoyed by any banjo player at any playing level.

Note: For suggestions on how to use this book for each playing level – refer to the *Foreword* on page 5.

Lesson 1: Left Hand Shapes
Shape #1 -- The "D7" Shape
Demonstrated with Cripple Creek

THERE ARE ONLY 3 BASIC LEFT HAND "SHAPES" and these are used over & over in every song you play.

If you will think about the patterns held with your left hand, it will be much easier to play a song in the melodic style than if you simply learn the song note by note. The left hand often works with certain "shapes" when a song is played on the banjo. In traditional bluegrass, the left-hand "shapes" are based upon chord positions. In the melodic style the shapes are scale positions, using only 2 fingers, and are drawn from the scale upon which the song is based. The same shape may be held in different areas of the fingerboard when playing a song in the melodic style. For example, *Cripple Creek,* which follows, uses Shape #1 throughout.

In the melodic style, only 3 basic left hand shapes are held by the left hand. Each *shape* involves holding down two adjacent strings with two left fingers. This forms the "shape" which can be held in different locations on the fingerboard to play songs in this style. These three shapes are drawn from scale positions in the G major scale.

The basic shapes will be referred to as *Shapes 1, 2, & 3. Each is* also referred to by the chord "shape" to which it is related.

SHAPE #1 -- THE "D7" SHAPE:

A very common left-hand shape used in the melodic style is formed exactly like the "D7" chord, which is a basic left-hand position most people learn as a beginner. This movable left-hand shape is held by the left index and middle fingers on two adjacent strings.   i.e. See *Cripple Creek* on the following page.

NOTE: Hold two notes at the same time, as you would a chord, even though the notes are to be picked one at a time.

SHAPE #1 on the Fingerboard
NOTE: This shape moves to different areas of the fingerboard while the left index and middle fingers will hold the same shape.

(can be moved to different (adjacent) strings and locations)

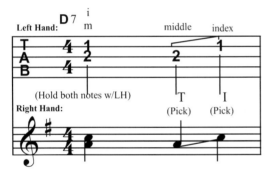

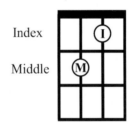

COMMON LOCATIONS FOR THE "D7" Shape in the Melodic Style:

The following are the most common fingerboard locations for this left-hand shape when a song is played in the Key of G. As you can see, this is a movable shape which is played on 2 adjacent strings. The left-hand fingering appears above the tab.
Bracket indicates: **Hold both notes with the left hand, then pick the notes separately with the right hand.**

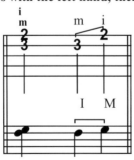
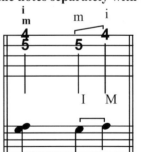
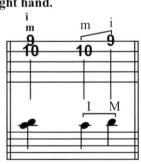

NOTES:
1.) In the D7 shape, the left *index* finger is on the string closest to the floor; the left *middle* finger is on the string closest to the ceiling.
2.) In the following arrangement for *Cripple Creek.,* the D7 chord shape is used by the left hand throughout the entire arrangement. In the traditional bluegrass style, the left hand holds chord positions. When playing a song in the "Melodic Style, the shapes are from the scale line.
3.) The above left-hand locations will be used in almost every song in this book. These positions are based upon the locations of these notes in the G major scale, which is the basis for songs played in the Key of G.
4.) Notice that *Cripple Creek* uses the Forward Reverse Roll in each measure with the right hand: TIMT MITM.
5.) FOR FURTHER STUDY OF SHAPE #1: See *Katy Hill* and *Sally Goodin'* for more songs based almost entirely upon the D7 chord shape.

Standard G Tuning: Key of G
Key of A: Capo 2nd fret

Cripple Creek

Measure Numbers are located below each measure,
for following the repeats, and substituting the licks at the bottom.
Brackets = hold both notes before picking.
Fingerboard diagram = above the bracket & left hand fingering = L.H. Shape

TRACK 6

Track 7: Slow
Track 8: Fast

The Left Hand: The following arrangement for *Cripple Creek* uses only Shape 1, the *"D7" shape,* with the left hand throughout Part A and Part B and should be fairly easy to play. Hold two notes at the same time with the left middle and index fingers, as you would a chord. This creates a shape which moves down the fingerboard to different frets as you play the song.

The Right Hand: plays the *Forward Reverse Roll* Pattern for each measure: **TIMT MITM.**

Remember to play Part A twice before playing Part B (twice).

Note: Left hand fingering is above the tab in difficult areas. Right hand fingering, when indicated, will be below the tab.

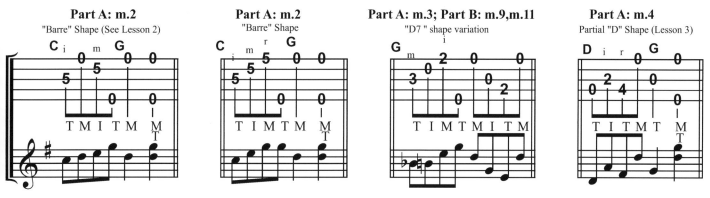

TRACK 9

Alternate Measures -- to be substituted in the arrangement above:

The above arrangement is also presented in the *You Can Teach Yourself Banjo*, as an introduction to the melodic style of 3-finger picking. Once you know this arrangement, substitute one or more of the following alternate measures in the arrangement above for the corresponding measure number(s). These provide a preview of additional left-hand melodic *shapes* to be presented in lessons which follow. (Left-hand fingering is above the tab. The new shapes will be discussed in Lessons 2 & 3.)

Part A: m.2	**Part A: m.2**	**Part A: m.3; Part B: m.9, m.11**	**Part A: m.4**
"Barre" Shape (See Lesson 2)	"Barre" Shape	"D7" shape variation	Partial "D" Shape (Lesson 3)

Notes: _____

This tune is usually performed with the capo on the 2nd fret, so the banjo is playing in the Key of A, as most fiddle and mandolin players play *Cripple Creek* in the Key of A. The capo shortens the banjo strings, so the actual pitches will be in the Key of A.

Lesson 2: Shape #2 - Melodic "Barre" Shape
Demonstrated with Blackberry Blossom

The second movable shape commonly held by the left hand in the melodic style, is based upon the *Barre Shape*. Two fingers are placed on the same fret on adjacent strings in the melodic style.

One finger may barre across the fret as with a 'barre chord' in the traditional bluegrass style, but often an open string will be included in the right hand picking in the melodic style, so this is not always possible.

*Note: The choice of left-hand fingers may vary for this position or shape, based upon what is played before and what is played after these two notes. Where possible, put the two left fingers down at the same time.

Hint: the left index & middle fingers are often recommended for the inside strings (2nd & 3rd strings) in this shape.

NOTE: Hold two notes at the same time, as you would a chord,
even though the notes are to be picked one at a time.

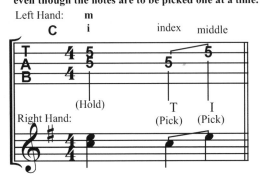

SHAPE #2 on Fingerboard
Can be moved to different (adjacent) strings & locations

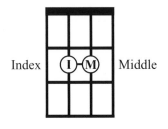

Index — Middle

("Barre") SHAPE #2 on 2 strings

(or "barre" one finger (i) over both strings)

COMMON LOCATIONS FOR THE Melodic "Barre" Shape:
Hold the 2 notes like a chord with the left hand, before picking the strings.

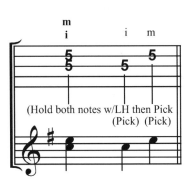

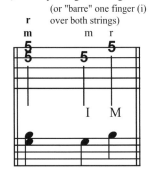

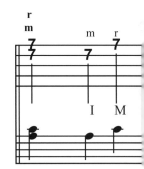

NEW "D7" Shape Locations:
Notice that Shape #1, the "D7" shape, is also an important left-hand shape throughout Blackberry Blossom.

Two additional "D7" locations appear in the following arrangement when an A chord is indicated.

The two new locations are demonstrated below (last 2 examples of the D7 shape.)

Normally, the chord to follow these positions when used for the A chord, will be the D chord.

Review: G scale tone locations using Shape #1 - the "D7" Shape:
Move the left fingers down the fingerboard in the same "shape" to the designated fret numbers.

New: D7 shape locations: (A chor
(See the Alt lick for m.4 in *Blackberry Blossom*)

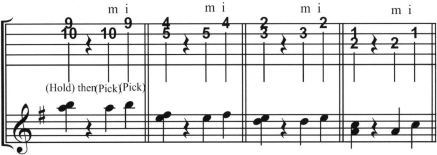

Notes:_____For further Study using the Barre Shape - see *Fisher's Hornpipe.*

G Tuning - Key of G

Measure Numbers appear under the staff.
Brackets = hold both notes before picking.
( ) = optional

Blackberry Blossom

Track 12: Slow
Track 13: Fast

Blackberry Blossom **is a popular "fiddle tune" among all bluegrass musicians and is fun to play on the banjo.** It helps when learning a song, to look for patterns *ahead of time.*

Left Hand: Before playing through this, try to identify the occurrences of the two left-hand shapes, (#1 "D7" shape & #2 "Barre" shape) discussed on the previous page. Move your left fingers to these positions, holding 2 notes at a time as you play through this arrangement. Note: Left-hand fingering is indicated above the tab. The bracket = hold both notes before picking.

Right Hand: Try to find familiar right-hand roll patterns as you play through this, also. Notice that m.1 & m.5 use the *Forward Roll, T I M T I M T I* and m.2, m.3, m.6 & m.7 use the *Forward Reverse Roll TIMT MITM.* Although the right hand does not necessarily work from roll patterns in the melodic style, roll patterns may be evident if you look for them.

Play Part A two times. Then, play Part B two times. Many fiddle tunes are divided into 2 parts: Part A and Part B.

NOTES: _____

*1.) See the Alternate Licks for a substitute A chord lick for m. 4 above. See "Fisher's Hornpipe" for more practice with Shape #2.

2.) The backup chords in measures 7 and 31 can be played as written, (C - G) or as G then C. Either way will sound fine with the above arrangement.

Alternate Measures
for Blackberry Blossom
Substitute in the Arrangement for the corresponding measure number(s).

Note: The dotted line between 2 measures indicates these may also be played together.

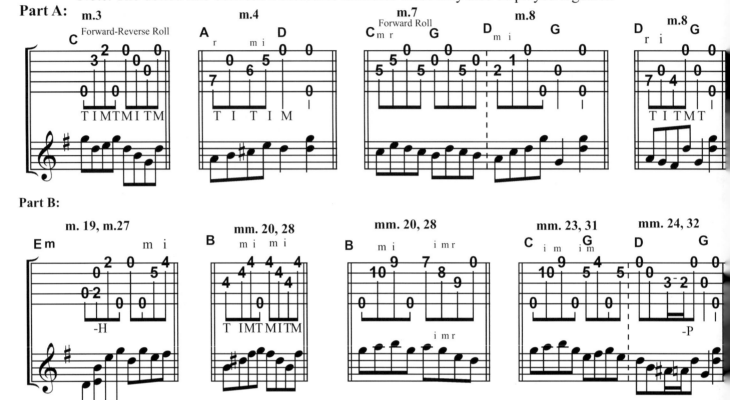

Lesson 3: Shape #3 - The "Partial D" Shape
Demonstrated with Fisher's Hornpipe

Shape #3, also called the "Partial 'D'" shape, completes the three most common 2-finger left-hand patterns which are held when playing in the 3-finger melodic style with the right hand. This third shape is based upon the left-hand fingering positions on the 3rd and 4th strings (bass strings) from the full "D" chord shape. In the melodic style, this is a shape which can be applied to other strings in different fretboard locations and works for other chords, depending upon where the left fingers are placed. Reminder: Whenever possible, place both left fingers on the designated strings at the same time.

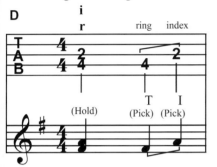

SHAPE#3 on Fingerboard

Can be moved to different adjacent strings and locations. Notice the shape skips a fret between the notes.

("Partial D") SHAPE #3

(on 2 adjacent strings)

COMMON LOCATIONS FOR THE "Partial D" Shape #3
Hold the 2 notes like a chord with the left hand, before picking the strings.

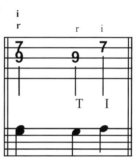
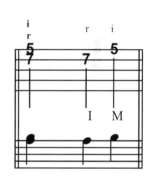

EXERCISES Connecting the Shapes:
Using Shapes 1, 2, & 3

For Practice: **Play through each of the following exercises (i.e. 5 times) in a row without pausing.** These include all three left-hand shapes covered so far. Exercise 1 begins with shape #1 (D7 shape), moves to shape #2 ("partial barre"), then to Shape #3 (partial D shape"). These are the seven notes in the G major scale, from the highest to the deepest pitch. Exercise 2 plays the G major scale in the opposite direction, also connecting all three shapes with the left hand. Exercise 3 uses only shape #3, the partial D shape, with the left hand. When possible, hold 2 down notes at a time with the left hand, in the designated "shape."

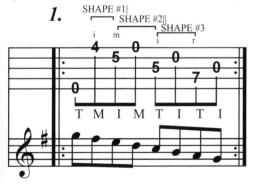
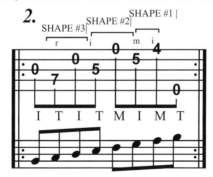

NOTES: _____

1.) Exercises 1 & 2 play all of the notes in the G Major Scale. These notes and left-hand positions are the basis for many songs played in the Melodic Style. i.e Notice the resemblance of Exercise 3 to the basic motif for *Orange Blossom Special.*

2.) Notice that *Fisher's Hornpipe* on the following page uses all three left-hand shapes. Which shape does it use the most?

( ) = optional
G Tuning - Key of G
> = emphasize

Fisher's Hornpipe

Track 18: Slow
Track 19: Fast

Fisher's Hornpipe is a popular tune which utilizes each of the three primary shapes (2-finger positions) for the left hand. This melodic style arrangement works along the scale line for the G major Scale, yet also has a melodic quality which is chordal. In addition to using Shape #3, notice that Shape #2 -- the "Barre Shape." is used frequently in this arrangement. Notice that at the 5th fret, shape #2 is often played for the C chord, and at the 7th fret it is often used for the D chord (indicated above the tab.) Also, notice in m.7, you have the option of holding shape 3, or shape 1. **Before playing through this, look for each shape.** Eventually, you will recognize these left hand positions quickly and your left hand will naturally and automatically finger them correctly.

Play Part A twice (substitute Ending 2 the second time); then play Part B twice.

NOTES:_____

1.) *Notice that the chord symbols are located above the tab. It is common in fiddle tunes to see measures split between 2 different chords.
   Also, notice that an A chord occurs in the 4th measure of Part B. When this occurs in the Key of G, the A chord will be followed by a D chord.
2.) Notice which fret numbers are associated with the chord names. Eventually, you can substitute melodic licks into any song for the appropriate chord
3.) A new shape is used for the left hand in measure 18. This is like the open string area "C" chord shape.

Substitute Licks

Alternate Measures for Fisher's Hornpipe

Optional Licks: (Substitute for the measure indicated)

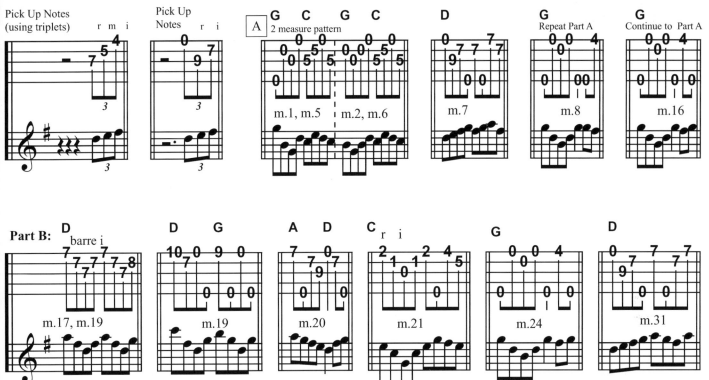

Note: When substituting a measure in the arrangement, the fingering should work smoothly with the measure before and after it. It may require changing a note, should it cause the same finger to be played twice in a row. It is fine to change any note(s) in the arrangement, as long as it sounds good to you, and plays easily.

Lesson 4: Choosing Shapes
Finding the Same Melody Notes in Different Places
Demonstrated With Devil's Dream

Bracket = Hold both notes
w/L.H. before picking separately.

Standard G Tuning:
Key of A: Capo 2nd Fret

It is important to also realize that the *same* two notes may be played on different strings in different locations on the fingerboard. When the *same* two notes played in one melodic scale shape are moved over to the next adjacent string(s), the "shape" will change. (If you hold the same shape with the left hand, the notes will be different.) The three basic melodic scale shapes work very much like chords when playing the "F," "D" and Barre Shapes for each chord letter name. The difference is that when working in melodic style, the shapes involve *two* melody notes or scale tones which can be moved to different strings as you go up the neck. Often the choice will be determined by which location is smoother for the right hand. Alternate Licks are also provided, so you can choose your own positions. Base your decision on the sound and ease of playability. The timbre (tone quality) also changes as you move up the neck.

EXAMPLES: Interchangeable Left-Hand Positions for the same notes:

The following shapes consist of exactly the same notes. The positions on the fingerboard are interchangeable and each is used often when these notes are played in a song. Notice in each example that the notes in Shape #1 (*"D7"* shape) use Shape #3 (the *Partial "D" Shape)* when moved over one string and up the neck to play the same notes.

The first example is a common choice in songs played in the melodic style.
Learn to interchange these above all others. Note: These are the 6th and 7th tones in the G scale line, (E and F#).

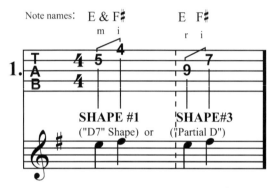

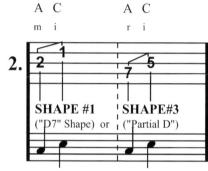

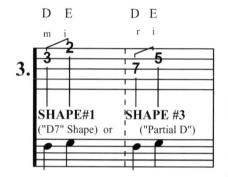

G Major Scale: Interchangeable shapes for the 6 & 7th notes.

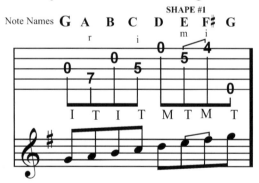

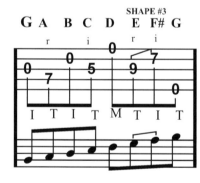

Devil's Dream: Measures 1 & 2 (choices) - Notice each example plays exactly the same notes.
The 2nd example uses the Mixed Roll with the Right Hand: T I T M T I T M)

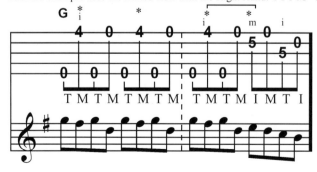

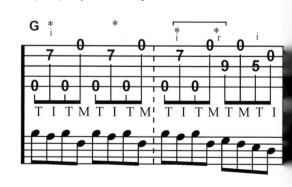

Standard G Tuning
Key of A: Capo 2nd Fret
( ) = optional

LESSON 4 Continued : Choosing Shapes

TRACK
22
Slow
Track 23: Fast

Devil's Dream

In the early 1960s, Bill Keith recorded *Devil's Dream* on the banjo in the melodic style as an instrumental tune with Bill Monroe's band. This tune became an instant hit with banjo players who were mesmerized by this relatively unknown picking style for 3-finger players. This tune is also a popular choice in jam sessions. This arrangement can be played as written, or you can use the alternate positions on the following page which use Shape #3 - the "Partial D" shape instead of Shape #1 - the "D7" shape. Notice how the melody travels up and down the (G) scale line.

Note: It is common for a fiddle tune to be performed in a specific key. *Devil's Dream* is almost always played in the Key of A by mandolin and fiddle players. Most banjo players play this tune in the Key of G, as written below, and place the capo across the 2nd fret of the banjo to convert the pitches to the Key of A.

Form: = Play Part A twice, then play Part B twice.

21

| measures with dashed bar line are often
played together.

Alternate Positions:
for Devil's Dream

Substitute select measures into the first arrangement, or create a second variation by playing all of the alternate measures continuously. Remember, you are the musician, so choose the positions that are most comfortable and/or sound the best to you.

Standard G Tuning:
Key of G
Bracket = hold both notes
before pick separately

Chapter 1: The 3 Left-Hand "Shapes"

 TRACK 25

Lesson 5: Review of Basic Melodic "Shapes"

The three left hand "shapes" covered in the previous lessons are movable shapes which are often held by the left hand when playing songs in the melodic style. Although the names relate to familiar chord shapes, these left hand patterns are scale shapes which can be played for different chords, depending upon the specific notes used in a specific area of a song.

Note: Hold the 2 notes at the same time with the left hand, like a chord, before picking the strings with the right hand. Each shape can be played on any two adjacent strings. In the Key of G, the following are the most common fingerboard locations for each shape. These are based upon the fingerboard locations of the two notes in the G major scale, which will be covered next.

1. SHAPE #1 - The "D7" Chord Shape:

The "D7" shape is based upon the left-hand fingering for the D7 chord in the open position. This is a standard left-hand shape used in the melodic style, which may be held/played in different areas of the fingerboard, as the major scale calls for this left-hand fingering. *Cripple Creek* uses this shape throughout. The left-hand fingering is indicated above the tablature. Also, see *Katy Hill* later on in this book for extensive use of this shape.

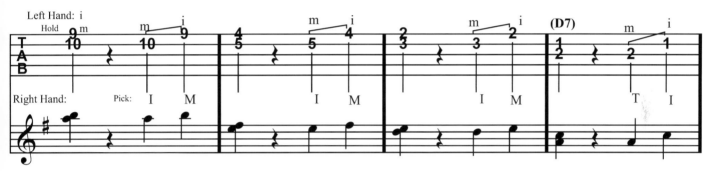

2. SHAPE #2 - The "BARRE" Chord Shape:

The second shape which is commonly held by the left hand is based upon the Barre Shape, where 2 fingers are placed on the same fret on adjacent strings. This position was presented with *Blackberry Blossom* (Lesson 2), and was also emphasized in *Fisher's Hornpipe* (Lesson 3). NOTE:There will be times where it is easier to fret 2 strings with one finger. Keep it smooth!

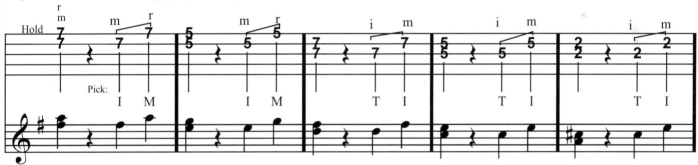

3. SHAPE #3 - The "PARTIAL D" Chord Shape:

The third basic shape is based upon the left-hand fingering positions held for the two deepest strings in the D chord shape. When moved to different fingerboard locations, the notes will change, but the left-hand shape is the same. This position was presented in *Fisher's Hornpipe,* and like the above shapes, will appear in almost every song played in the melodic style.

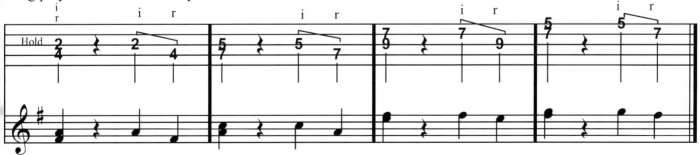

Lesson 6: The Melody & the "G" Major Scale Tones

Demonstrated with Flop Eared Mule

TRACK 26

When a song is played in the melodic style, almost every note is a melody note.

The G scale provides the set of notes used to play songs in the Key of G. This scale consists of only 7 tones, which repeat as you go up the fingerboard. The Key of G uses these tones for the melody *and* the chords. The order of the notes in each song depends upon the song and what the composer intended for the melody.

The 'G' Major Scale:

The G Major Scale consists of 7 tones played in alphabetical order starting with G. This repeats as you go up the fingerboard.

'G' Scale Tones on Different Strings - 3 Finger Style:

Notice the *left hand shapes* as you play through this scale.

The 'G' Major Scale: On One String

The distance on the fingerboard from one note to the next is like a phone number.:

The 'G' Scale - Melodic Style: **Play each successive note on a different string, using a different right-hand finger. (Hold the LH shapes.)**

These notes provide the basis for all songs which are played in the Key of G. Hold 2 left fingers at the same time when possible.

EXERCISES: 1.) Play the Ascending scale line x 5 without pausing.   2.) Play the Descending scale x 5. 3.) Play the scale up and back x 5.

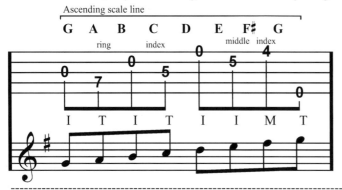

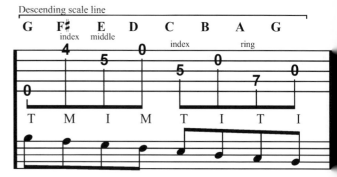

EXTENDING the *G* Scale Up the Fingerboard -- Melodic Style: Preview for the more advanced player.

The 7 tone names of the G Scale repeat as you play up the fingerboard. The pitches will be higher as you move to the next octave. It can also go down the fingerboard on the 4th string to the open 4th string, D, which is the deepest tone on the banjo. The G scale can begin and end with any tone in the scale, as long as these 7 notes are the only notes played.

The following scale line includes the melody notes used to play *Flop Eared Mule* on the next page*.   * = Extended scale

NOTES:_____

1.) The musical alphabet consists of only 7 letters: A B C D E F G. The basic G scale starts with G and sharps the F (♯ 7th tone).
   In songs, the melody uses these notes, but they will be placed according to the composer's intent. The chords also use these tones.
2.) In the Melodic 3-Finger Style, the scale tones are played on different strings so one right-hand finger does not have to pick a string twice in a row.
3.) The scale line can begin with any note; i.e. play A through A, using the same set of notes.
4.) If a different note appears in the song from the notes in the scale line, it is "borrowed" from a different scale.

( ) = optional or implied
Follow the Measure Numbers
for the repeats and alt. licks.

\> = accent - melody note

Flop Eared Mule

Flop Eared Mule demonstrates a melodic style arrangement which is played in the Key of G using the G scale tones. Using the two finger shapes with the left hand from the G scale, this tune should be fairly easy to play. Hint: pick out Shape #3 - the "Partial D" shapes in Part A, and Shape #1 - the "D7" shapes in Part B before you begin playing. Notice how the melody runs down, then up the G major scale line in the first four measures. Virtually every note played in the "melodic" style is a melody note; the scale line may begin with different notes when changing directions, based upon the melody. *Practice Tips:* Concentrate on the first four measures, first. These patterns recur throughout. If a passage seems difficult, isolate the measure(s) and play this area 5 times without hesitating, until you can play it without a mistake.

Form: Play Part A twice, then Part B once, *then* Part A once more to play the complete variation.

Notes:_____For anyone interested in music theory:

1.) Part B includes the A chord. Notice the shape with the left hand. This chord is often used in songs before the D chord.

2.) Part B moves into the Key of D, which uses the D scale tones. The D scale uses *exactly* the same notes as the G major scale, except the C is raised to a C♯, and the D scale begins with the D note instead of with the G note. This will be discussed and further demonstrated later in this course near the end of the book.

Substitute Licks for Flop Eared Mule

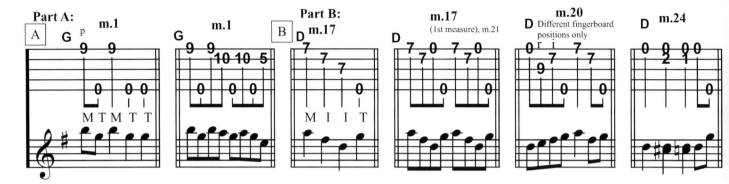

QUESTION: What left-hand *shapes* are used in m.20 above?

Answer: The Partial D Shape 3 in a new location, *and* Barre Shape 2.

The Melody for *Flop Eared Mule*

Compare the basic melody below with the first eight measures in the melodic style arrangement for *Flop Eared Mule* (Part A). In the arrangement on the previous page, the melody notes are indicated with accent marks (>) over the tab. Notice how the scale line is used as fill between the melody notes. (In m.3, the notes in parenthesis are optional positions on the fingerboard.)

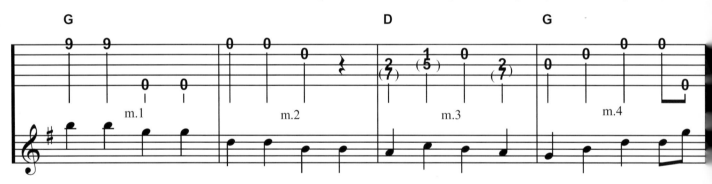

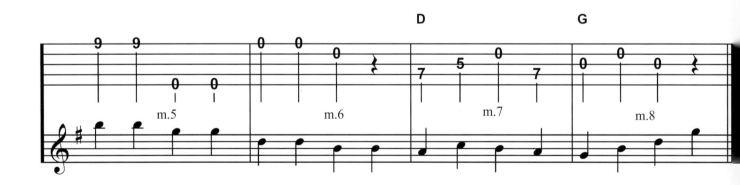

Lesson 7: Mini Scale Pattern #1
Demonstrated with Fire on the Mountain

THERE ARE FIVE "Mini" SCALE PATTERNS with 4 specific notes which are commonly used in the melodic style.
A "*Mini*" *Scale Pattern* **is a set or sequence of four** *specific notes* from the (G) scale line, which occurs over and over in many different songs. These will be presented one at a time in the following lessons. Once you learn Pattern #1, you will find it in almost every song you play. There are five specific scale "patterns," as noted above. **Each scale** *pattern consists of only 4 notes.* These patterns are *not* movable *shapes.* They are a set of specific notes. Keep in mind that each scale pattern = 1/2 of a measure or lick. (A "lick" contains 8 notes = 1 measure.)

'G' SCALE PATTERN #1:

Scale Pattern #1 is extremely common in songs played in the Key of G.
This set of notes is frequently played at the end of a phrase just before the open 3rd string, and is often played for the D chord, leading into the G chord. To hear the resolution, play the open 3rd string (G) after the last note in the pattern.
This pattern is played in m.4, m.8, m.12, m.16, and m.26 in *Fire on the Mountain.*)

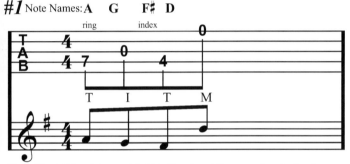

Note: The left hand does not hold both notes at the same time in the above sequence.

'G' Major Scale extended up the neck one note:
These are the notes which provide the basis for the melody notes in *Fire on the Mountain.*
Practice this scale line up and back until you can play it smoothly. Pattern #1 ends this exercise.

Compare measures 1 and 2 in *Fire On The Mountain* with the above scale line to see how the melodic style works with the 'G' Scale line. It is amazing to realize that there are only 7 different notes in this scale, and that an incredible number of different tunes have been written using these 7 notes. **Notice** that the opening measures for *Fire on the Mountain* start with the 5th note and work backwards down the scale line to the first note.

NOTES:_____

1.) When a fiddle tune is played in the melodic style, almost every note can be considered a melody note.
   If you try to sing it, these notes are what you might sing. However, these melodies can also be simplified by picking out the most important notes, especially on the "down" beats (the first beat in a measure.)
2.) By also looking for the simpler melody, it enables you to see where you might change an arrangement to use different scale patterns & licks. See the Substitute Licks for *Fire on the Mountain* for more on this.
*3.) There are three Left-Hand SHAPES AND there are five "Mini" Scale Patterns. It is important to distinguish between the three L.H. SHAPES introduced in Chapter 1 in Lessons 1-5, and the five "Mini" Scale Patterns, which are sets of *specific notes* which are often used in songs which are played in the Melodic Style, as discussed in Chapter 2.

G Tuning
Key of A -- Capo 2nd Fret

Fire on the Mountain

> = melody note

When playing this tune in the melodic style, virtually every note you play is a melody note.
The primary melody notes are indicated with an accent mark (>). Before you play through this arrangement for
Fire on the Mountain, look for the now familiar left-hand shapes and how the melody works up and down the
scale line. Also notice the occurrance of *Scale Pattern 1,* especially in m.4, and at the end of the song. This
set of notes is used in many different songs. (Scale Pattern #2 is also indicated as preparation for the next song.)
As the title indicates, this is a very peppy tune which should be played smoothly and up tempo.

FORM: Play Part A (mm.1-4) ***FOUR times*; then play Part B** *two times;* **then play Part C** *one time.*

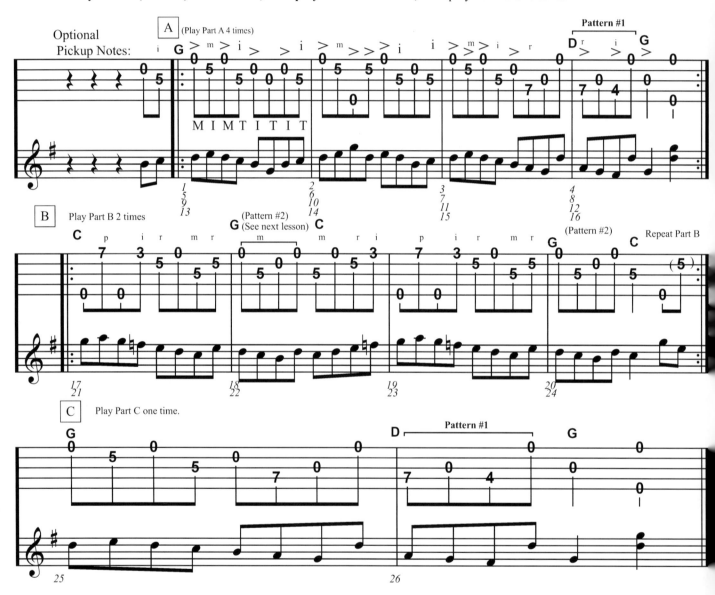

Notes:_____
1.) Part B, m.17 (first measure), the 4th fret on the 1st string (F♯ in the G scale) is lowered to the 3rd fret (F natural).
   This passage uses the C major scale tones, which will be covered later in this book. However, it is important to realize that *F* is the *only note*
   that is different between the G scale and the C scale. All the other notes are the same in both scales, and in songs played in the Keys of G & C.
   It strengthens the effect of the main tonality or key, when the song returns and ends in the original key.
2.) Once you have learned to play this song, place your capo on the 2nd fret every time you play it.
   Fire on the Mountain is traditionally played in the Key of A. Remember to compensate the 5th string the same distance (2 frets higher).

Substitute Licks: For Fire on the Mountain

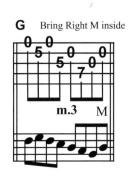

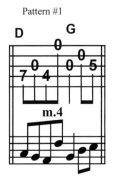

Sub. for m.4 the 4th time through Part A. Pattern #1

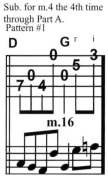

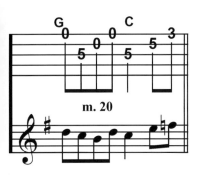

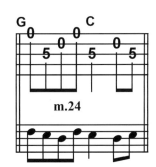

MELODY ONLY for PART A measures 1-4

Compare the melody below for *Fire on the Mountain* with the same measures in the melodic style arrangement and notice how the scale tones are inserted between the melody notes to connect them tonally.

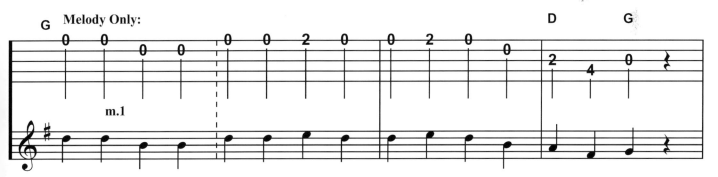

Melody in the Melodic Style:

Main melody notes indicated with >.

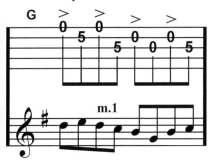

Notes may be moved or changed once you have the melody notes in place. One reason may be to make the passage smoother to play in the 3-finger style. Here, the 6th note is played with an open string. Make your choice and stay with it.

Lesson 8: Mini Scale Patterns #2 & #3
Also: How to Work Out a Melodic Style Arrangement
with Twinkle, Twinkle Little Star

TRACK
34

The melodic style works with 5 basic "scale patterns," in addition to working with the moveable shapes used by the left hand. Scale Pattern # 1 was introduced in the previous lesson with *Fire on the Mountain.* The following two patterns are also basic (G) "scale patterns" which occur frequently in the melodic style.
Reminder: The basic unit for a scale pattern consists of a set of *four specific notes from the G scale.*
These are *not movable* patterns. Instead, they are a combination of certain notes from the G scale.
Note: When two patterns are combined, they equal one measure of music. Usually, the 1st note of the pattern is a melody note for the song.

'G' SCALE PATTERNS #2 & #3

Scale Patterns #2 & #3 are circular scale patterns. In each group of four notes, the first and fourth notes are the same note. Each circular pattern goes up or down the scale line for three notes, then circles back to the beginning note. This often "stair steps" up or down the G scale in groups of four notes. Each four-note pattern may be played for a specific chord, or it may be combined with other patterns and applied to a different chord. The chords are implied, as these may work in a melodic run for other chords.
NOTE: Keep in mind that each scale pattern = 1/2 of a measure or a "lick." (See *Fire on the Mountain* for Scale Shape #1*.)

Twinkle, Twinkle Little Star: Working Out a Melodic 3-Finger Arrangement

The following demonstrates how to pick out the melody notes, then add notes as fill between the melody notes for measures 1 & 2 of *Twinkle Twinkle Little Star*, which is a familiar melody built with notes from the G scale. (See Lesson 6 for the G Major Scale.)
Example A = Melody Only; Example B = Adds Scale Pattern #3; Example C = Melodic Style.
Notice that the first note of each scale pattern is a main melody note in the melodic version.
Note: Concentrate on "scale patterns" #1 - #3 and how they are used in songs. (Patterns #4 & #5 are included at the end; these will be covered next lesson.)

A.) THE MELODY ONLY mm. 1 & 2
Find the Melody Notes for mm 1 & 2 from the G Scale in the melodic positions:

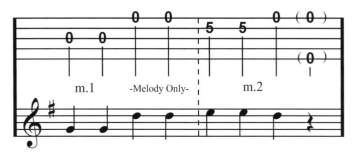

B.) MELODY with PATTERN #3

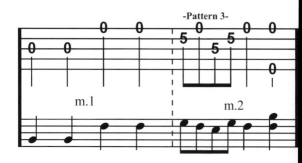

C.) ADDING SCALE PATTERNS #2 & #3 to the Melody

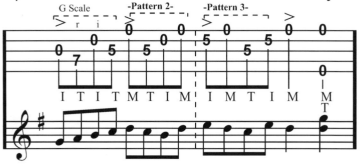

For the Advanced Player: mm 3&4 w/Preview of Patterns 4 & 5

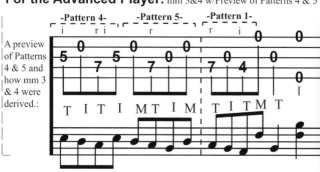

Notes:_____ 1.) Measures 3 & 4 use Scale Patterns 4 and 5: Notice that pattern #5 uses the middle finger on the inside string (2nd string).

G Tuning - Key of G
Capo 2 for Key of A
> = melody note

Twinkle, Twinkle Little Star

TRACK
35
Slow
Track 36: Fast

Twinkle, Twinkle Little Star **is the familiar tune which is also used for the alphabet song.**

To play this in the melodic style, the spaces between the melody notes are filled in with notes from the G scale.

Many of the same melodic style patterns appear in different songs. The more tunes you learn to play in this style, the easier these patterns will become. You can simply learn this song and enjoy playing it, or continue on for more tips on how the scale patterns work and are combined to create a melodic style arrangement. Notice that mm. 1-4 are repeated in mm. 9-12. Also, mm. 5 & 6 are played again for mm. 7 & 8. Practice these measures as a 2-measure unit.

It helps to isolate the patterns into 4 note units. Notice that these start and end with the same scale tone as they cycle down the scale line. These are based upon the "circular" G major scale, which will be discussed later on in this book. For now, learn the sound and the fingering patterns. Practice each pattern on the previous page over & over until it feels natural to play it.

The first note of each 4-note group is a prominent melody note. Other melody notes may be implied in order to work with the scale patterns in the melodic style, (indicated in parenthesis).

ALSO: *Notice the left-hand shapes* as they form naturally while the melody works with the scale patterns. It helps to identify the shape and fret location with the chord being played, as they often work with the same chord in other songs.

*Note: In measures 3 & 6, the right middle finger picks the 2nd string. See the substitute lick at the bottom of the following page if this is difficult.

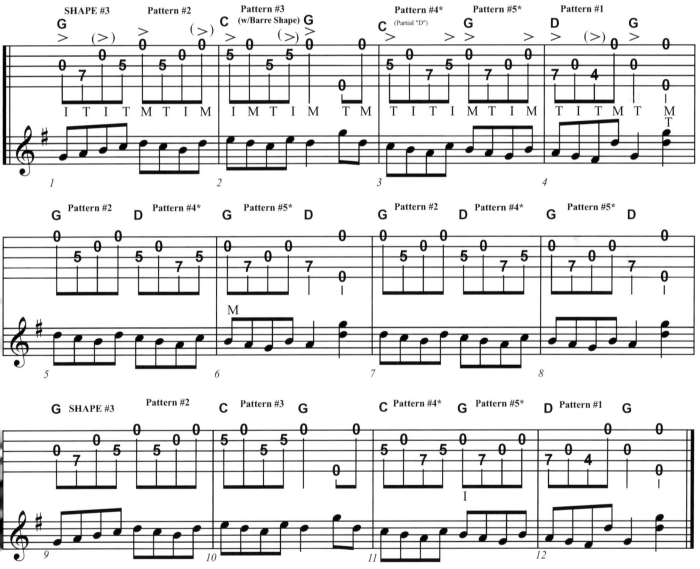

NOTES:_____

1.) Look for these patterns in new songs to make them easier to play. Find these in the songs you have learned so far too.

2.) The above patterns are often combined to be played as 2-measure patterns. Notice that the final 2 measures are a rolling melodic pattern which is part of the circular scale. This is a popular ending for tunes played in the melodic style.

3.) Notice the chord for which each 4-note pattern applies. These can be used for the same chords in many different songs, especially when the melody note is the first note of the pattern.

Twinkle Twinkle Little Star - #2
Alternate Variation

Measures 1 & 2 place the true melody notes in the accurate positions rhythmically within the measure.
The notes used to fill the spaces between the melody notes are "chromatic" tones on either side of the melody note, (indicated with a sharp point over the note.) For fun, substitute these examples for measures 1 and 2 of the arrangement on the previous page, and vice versa. Note: In m. 6, the right middle finger picks the open 2nd string. Substitute the open 1st string if this is difficult, in order to learn the song, but keep practicing using this finger on the inside string. Note: For practice, look for repeated patterns as you play through this. Find the three left-hand shapes and also look for scale patterns #1 - #3. Also, look for patterns with the right hand. Notice that m.3 = forward roll pattern: TIMTIMTI.

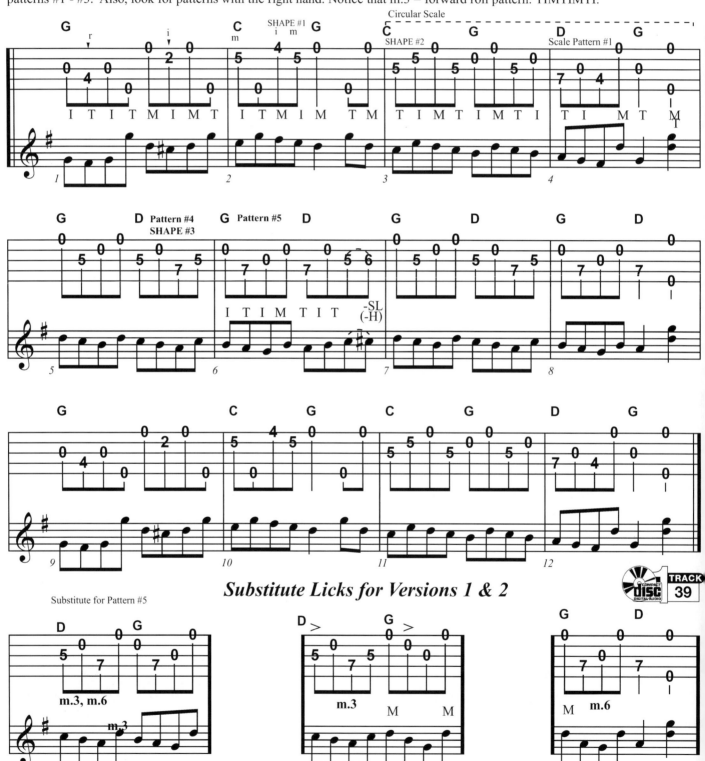

Substitute Licks for Versions 1 & 2

TRACK 39

Substitute for Pattern #5

Lesson 9: Mini Scale Patterns #4 & #5

Demonstrated with Redwing

This lesson introduces Scale "Patterns" #4 & #5 to complete the introduction of the five "basic" 4-note scale patterns. These patterns should become very familiar as you play more songs in this style. There are countless additional patterns, and combinations of patterns. The important point is to learn to recognize patterns of notes which occur repeatedly in one song, as well as in general. This makes the song easier to play and provides you with tools for working out your own arrangements in the melodic style.

To remember a pattern, look for something else identifiable like a left-hand shape, or the chord for which it is used.

i.e. The notes belonging to Pattern #4 involve holding the Partial D shape with your left ring and index fingers. When you come across this pattern in a new song, it will be easy to play. Pattern #5 involves picking the 2nd string with the right middle finger, which is fairly common in the melodic style. This will be effortless in a song if you are already comfortable picking the inside string with your right middle finger. *Keep in mind that each basic scale pattern = 1/2 of a measure or a lick.*

'G' Scale Patterns #4 & # 5

(First previewed in *Twinkle Twinkle Little Star.*)

Pattern #4
(Hold Partial "D" SHAPE #3)

Pattern #5

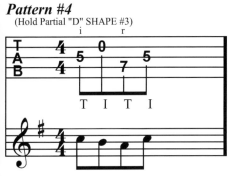

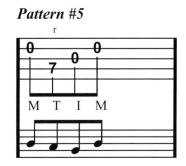

Exercise: Patterns 2, 4, 5, 1 combined

This combination forms a 2-measure "lick" which can be used in many songs for the G and/or D chord.
The last four measures of *Redwing* use this sequence to draw the chorus to a close.
The first note of each scale pattern creates a scale line leading to the open third string (G chord tone.)

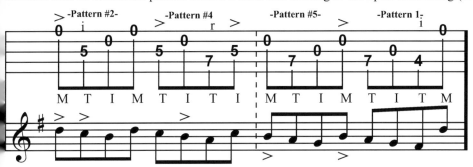

Preview: **The Circular Scale** for playing in the melodic style. Because melodies frequently work

along scale lines, and because melodic licks are often derived from the circular scale, this is an important scale for playing in the melodic style. The following exercise is a combination of four-note scale patterns like those presented above.

The first note of each four-note pattern is a G major scale tone which steps down (or up) the G scale line 2 notes, then "circles" back to the same pitch as the first note. The scale line can begin and end with any note. i.e for the C chord, it might begin with a C note or another note belonging to the C chord. When used in a song, the pattern will usually begin with an important melody note.

To make this easier to play, notice the basic left-hand shapes as you play through this. Also, find the 4-note scale patterns #1- #5.

Circular Scale:

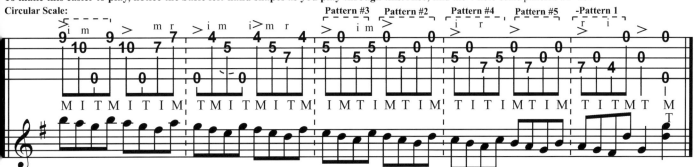

G Tuning: Key of G
( ) = optional

Redwing

TRACK
41
Slow

Track 42: Fast

Notice how the following melodic style arrangement works with the G scale line. A melody note begins the first measure for each new chord, and continues with the G major scale tones moving up and down to capture the main melody notes. The "scale" *patterns* which were discussed on the previous page are used in Part B. (mm.21-24). As you work through this tune, also look for the familiar left-hand "shapes." Measure 7 includes an A chord pattern, which uses the "D7" shape #1. Hints: hold the left ring finger on the 7th fret for m.5-7. Also, look for patterns by chord. For example, what do you play for the C chord?

FORM: Play the verse through Ending 1, mm.7 & 8; repeat the verse but substitute the 2nd ending, mm.15-16; play the chorus.

NOTES: _____

1.) This tune includes an A chord, just before the D chord. This is common for many songs in the Key of G (i.e. *Blackberry Blossom*.) When a chord is borrowed from another key like this one is, you can simply hold the chord with your left hand and play a roll pattern with the right hand, or you can play a melodic pattern for the chord. The purpose of the A chord in the Key of G, is to go to the D chord.

Substitute Licks *for Redwing*

Substitute each measure below in the arrangement for *Redwing* with the corresponding measure number.
It is fun to combine measures which are in sequence, and substitute these as a group for a different effect.
The dotted bar line = 2 measure "lick"

35

Lesson 10: Review - Mini (4-Note) Scale "Patterns

The Five Basic Mini Scale "Patterns"

Each scale pattern below is a specific set of notes from the G Scale commonly used in the melodic style.
Each pattern consists of 4 notes = 1/2 measure of music. These can be combined in many different ways, depending upon the melody and the chords for the song. (The chord indicated would apply to the first note of the pattern.)
When patterns are combined, the first pattern chosen will usually start with a tone belonging to the chord in the song.

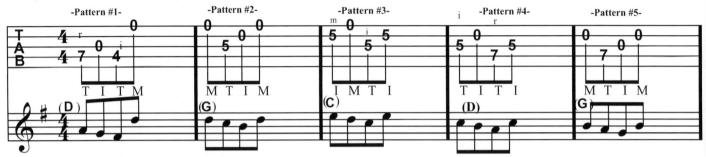

Combining Scale Patterns

The first ex. below forms a popular 2-measure pattern by combining Patterns 2-4-5-1 from above. This 2 mm. "lick" is often used at the end of a section for the "D" chord, leading to the open "G" chord. The second ex. = 3 measures.

Patterns 2 - 4- 5- 1

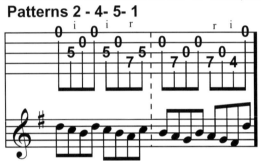

Patterns 3 - 2 - 4 - 5 - 1 (3 measure pattern)

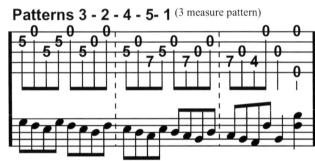

Circular Scale Patterns

Circular Scales provide the basis for many melodic style licks and patterns used in songs. The following is a basic descending circular pattern. All of the notes are from the G major scale line. Notice that the 1st and 4th notes are the same tone in each four note group. Visualize a circular staircase - walk down (or up) three steps (notes)- then go back to the 1st step (note); move down (or up) one step and repeat this sequence. (See *Redwing* for more.)

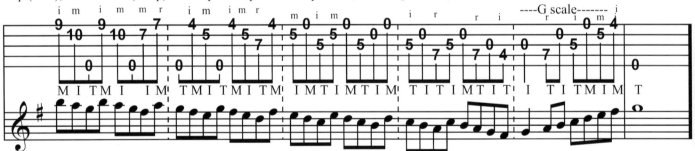

Preview: *The 'G' Major Scale starting from the lowest note on the fingerboard up to the 10th fret*

The scale line can begin and end with any note. i.e for the C chord, it might begin with a C note or another note belonging to the C chord. Make an exercise of this by looping it several times up and back without stopping.
Notice that the left thumb frets the 10th fret. Note: The basic G major scale positions from Lesson 6 are included in the brackets.

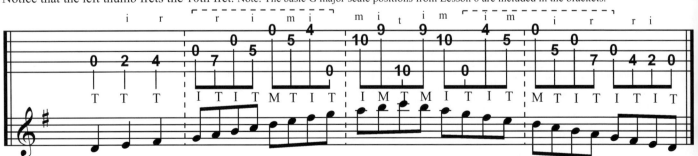

Lesson 11: Adding an Introduction
Demonstrated with Bill Cheatham
Also: Placing The Melody Notes in a Melodic Style Pattern

It is often effective to play a brief introduction before beginning the actual performance of a song.
This "revs" up the audience for what is to come, sets the beat for the song, and signals the band, when playing with others, when to "come in." The following is a popular introduction for banjo players to use with fiddle tunes. (When playing with others, this is usually played as a solo by the banjo, before the band begins.)
Note: The *pickup notes* at the end of the introduction lead directly into m.1 of the actual song.

BASIC INTRODUCTION (4 measures)   *pickup notes

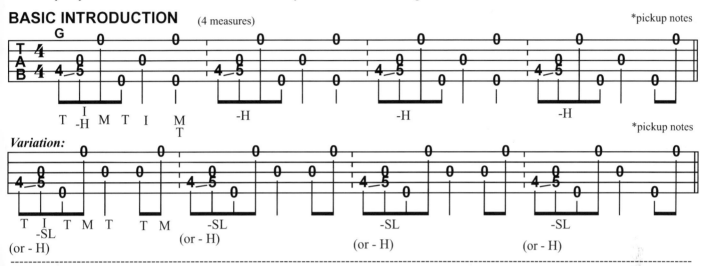

PLACING THE MELODY Notes in a Melodic Style Pattern versus a Bluegrass Roll Pattern:
The following examples contrast placing the melody notes in a bluegrass roll pattern, versus placing them in a melodic style scale pattern. The melody for Part B of *Bill Cheatham* goes up the G major scale line from the 5th note (D) up to the 8th note (G). There are many different options for incorporating the melody into an arrangement.

MELODY ONLY: Opening melody notes and chord names in Part B.

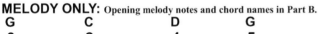

BLUEGRASS STYLE ROLL: MIMT MIMT

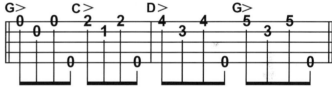

MELODIC STYLE with Basic G Scale Pattern
The melody note is the 1st note of each group of four eighth notes. Notice this forms a 2-measure "circular" scale pattern.

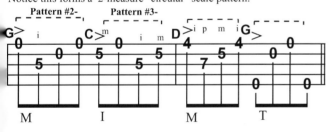

Variation #1: MELODIC STYLE with FORWARD ROLL
*Each melody note may also be moved to a different position or beat to accommodate a roll pattern for the right hand. This makes it easier and smoother to play, and often adds syncopation to the rhythmic effect.

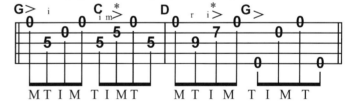

Variation #2: MELODIC STYLE with Chord & Scale Tones
The notes in each pattern may be chord tones belonging to the indicated chord, or they may use the scale line up, down and/or around the melody note. It is fun to experiment. Compare this with the above example.

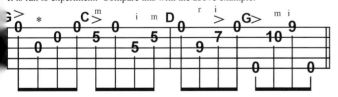

Variation #3: MELODIC STYLE with BACKWARD ROLL
The right-hand patterns may be alternated. Although the bluegrass rolls often work well, there is no definitive melodic style right-hand roll pattern.

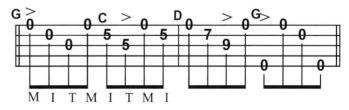

Notes: 1.) In the Melodic Variations above, the Forward Roll AND the Backward Roll start with the middle finger of the right hand -- due to the melody note's string location. 2.) Each of the above 2-measure examples are interchangeable in the first two measures for Part B in *Bill Cheatham* (mm. 17-18).

G Tuning - Key of G
Key of A = Capo 2nd fret

Bill Cheatham

Track 46 Slow
Track 47: Fast

The introduction can be used for many different fiddle tunes. You can slide from 4 to 5 on the fourth string, or hammer, whichever feels and sounds the best to you. The last two notes are pick up notes leading into Part A.

Look through the tab. and find the familiar left-hand shapes. Also, start to identify what pattern is played for a particular chord. Part B, m. 18 includes the left hand over the tab, to make this easy to play. The two measure examples on the previous page can also be substituted for mm.17 & 18 in Part B.

In measure 2 of Part A, the right middle finger comes "inside" to pick the 2nd string.* Substitute the 1st string, if this is difficult, but keep practicing this technique, as it will become easier with time. This is a melody note, and should be included if possible. (This is scale pattern #5 introduced in a previous lesson.)

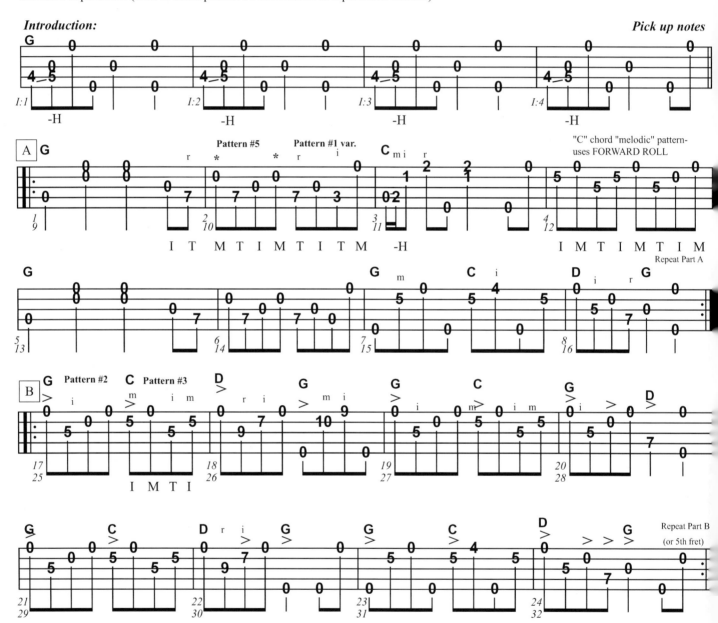

NOTES:

1.) In Part A, the last note of m.2 is played on the 3rd fret of the 4th string, instead of on the usual 4th fret. This lowers the F♯ note to an F♮.
   The purpose is to lead the ear of the listener into the C chord.
2.) The pattern played in Part A, measures 7 & 8 use a variation of the pattern used in *Blackberry Blossom* (Lesson 2) for these measure numbers.
3.) Notice in Part B: the 1st, 3rd and 5th measures play the same pattern.
4.) Also, notice the four-note pattern used for each chord indicated. These will apply in any song for the corresponding chord.
5.) Look for the "C" chord patterns. These are used for the C chord in many different songs played in this style.

Substitute Patterns & Licks for Bill Cheatham:

NOTE: Adding a chromatic* tone - A chromatic tone occurs between two notes of the major scale line. It can add interest and motion to a passage, altering an expected scale tone by raising or lowering it one fret. This changes the scale tone to a chromatic tone.* Substitute the first example in measure 4 of Part A to hear how this changes the effect.

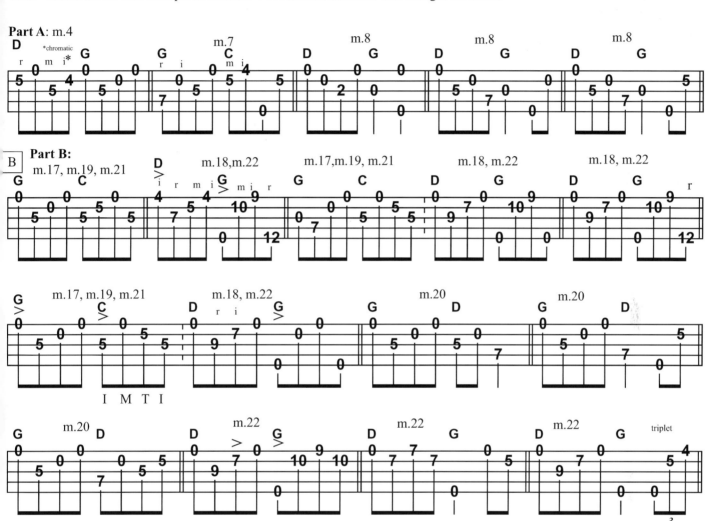

OPTIONAL ENDING: Add after m.32, or substitute for indicated measures.

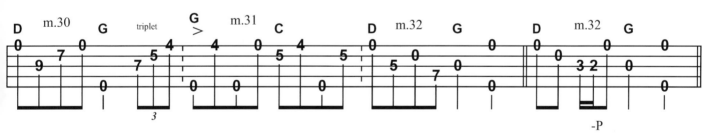

TRACK 49

Lesson 12: Pick Up Notes & Triplets
With The Big Sandy River

An effective way to begin a fiddle tune on the banjo is to play a "triplet" for the pick up notes, which adds excitement and energy right from the beginning. Remember, this is just a partial measure which begins with the last beat of the measure. *A triplet consists of three notes* which are played in the same amount of time 2 standard eighth notes are played. > = emphasize (Accent or emphasize the first note of the triplet.)

TRI - po - let

To play a triplet, the three notes are played in the same amount of time 2 regular eighth notes are played; the last note of the triplet is immediately followed by another note, (see ex. 2). The following examples can be used as pickup notes for any song which starts with the open 5th string in the first measure. (i.e. *Blackberry Blossom, Devil's Dream, Fisher's Hormpipe, Cuckoo's Nest,* and more.)

HINT: Say *"Tri - Po - Let"* as you play the notes in the triplet, emphasizing the 1st note (Tri-).

PICK UP NOTES with a Triplet

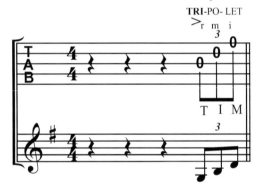

Play the note *after* the triplet without a pause or break in the rhythm.

Variations: The notes in the above triplet may also be played as follows when used as pickup notes before the open 5th string:

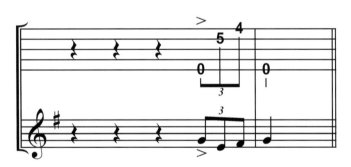

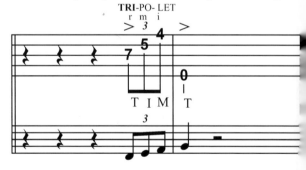

Optional:_____
If the triplet is difficult for you to play, it is also acceptable to play two eighth notes using the 2nd and 3rd notes only. However, continue to practice the triplet technique, as eventually it will be easy to play.

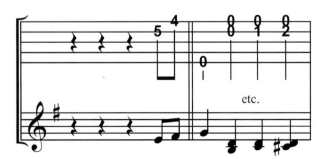

Notes: _____
1.) A triplet may also be used within a song.
Often this occurs at the end of a phrase to lead into the next phrase.
See m.4 in *The Big Sandy River.*
(Also, this would work in *Blackberry Blossom,* m. 4 for the last beat. And see *The Cuckoo's Nest,* m.8 when repeating Part A.)

Standard G Tuning
Key of A: Capo 2nd fret

The Big Sandy River

Slow

Track 51: Fast

The pick up notes should only be played to begin the song. When repeating the section, these should be omitted. Accent the first note of the triplet and play the three notes in the same amount of time you would play two eighth notes.
FORM: In the traditional fiddle tune form, play Part A through m.8 (1st ending); Repeat Part A- skip 1st ending (m.8) & substitute 2nd ending (m.16.) Then, continue with Part B.
See the alternate lick options to substitute in the appropriate measure(s) at the end of the arrangement.

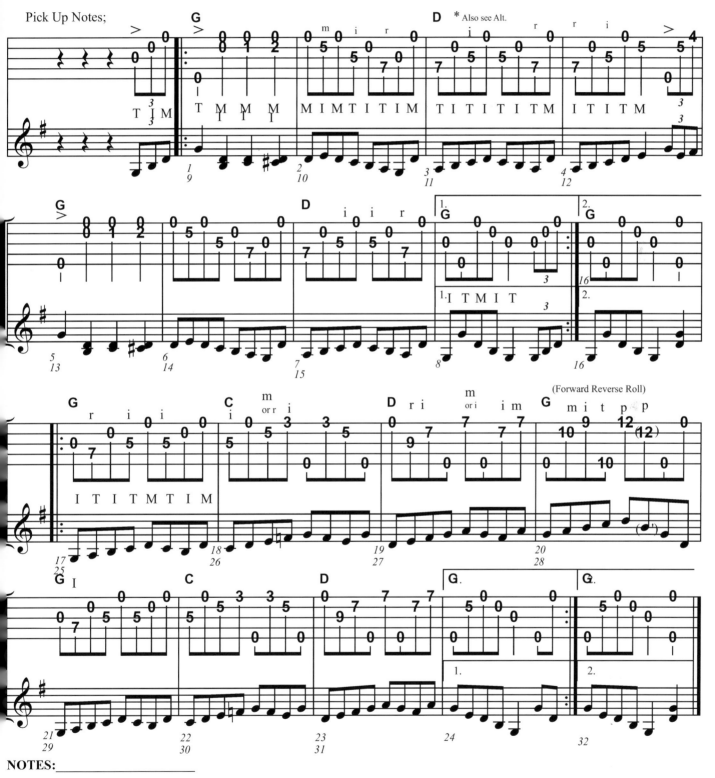

NOTES:_____

1.) In Part, B, each measure plays the scale tones belonging to the chord indicated.
   i.e. m.17 = G scale tones; m.18 = C scale tones; m.19 = D scale.

Optional Introduction:

Introduction for Fiddle Tunes (4 Measures) + Triplet as Pick Up into the Song:

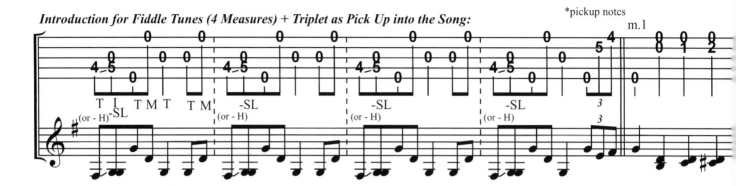

Substitute Licks for The Big Sandy River:

Pickup Notes
Substitute each pattern in the above arrangement for the indicated measure(s).

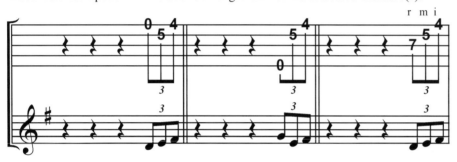

Part A:
When Part A is repeated, measures 3 & 4 become measures 11 & 12. Banjo players often substitute different patterns when repeating Part A in order to add variety. Notice how each pattern below changes the overall effect.

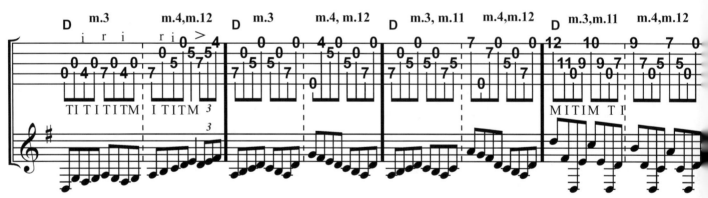

Part B:
Measures 17- 20 and 25-28

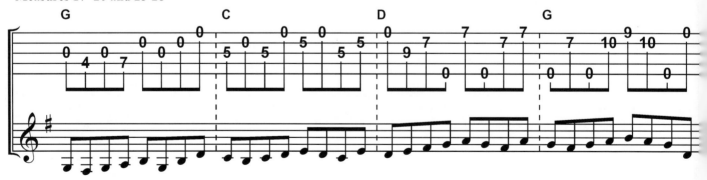

Lesson 13 - Fretting the 5th String
With Whiskey Before Breakfast
Also: Using The Circular Scale Pattern

> = accent

⌐—⌐ = hold before picking

By now, the melodic fingerboard "shapes" and basic scale "patterns" for the Key of G should be familiar and the arrrangement for *Whiskey Before Breakfast* should be fairly easy and a lot of fun to play. Part B of *Whiskey Before Breakfast* includes three additional techniques which have not yet been discussed in depth. Each of these is also a fairly common occurrence in the melodic style.

1.) FRETTING the 5th STRING with the left hand: When playing up the neck in the melodic style, the 5th string is often fretted in order to include a melody note or play a scale pattern. In Part B, the second measure (m.18,) the left *ring* finger frets the 5th string at the 12th fret. In measure 20, the left *thumb* frets the 10th fret (melody note.)
When fretting the 5th string, use the left finger which is most natural for ease of playability.

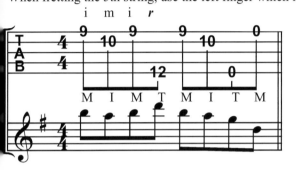

2.) RHYTHM - A commonly-used *syncopated rhythm* using an eighth note + quarter note = short - long:
See mm.17 & 19 in *Whiskey Before Breakfast*. This rhythm also occurs in *Big Scioty* and other tunes in this book.
Hold or sustain the quarter note twice as long as the eighth note. In the ex. to the right, sustain but do not pick the note in parenthesis. This is a popular rhythm in bluegrass style arrangements as well as in the melodic style.

As written with
quarter + eighth notes:

The *same* rhythm written
with only eighth notes:

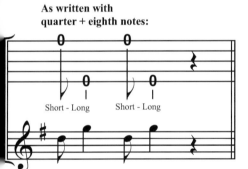

3.) CIRCULAR SCALE Pattern(s) - See Lesson 9 *(Redwing)* and Lesson 10 (Review) for an introduction to this scale type.
The same circular scale pattern can be played in different songs for the same chords with a different effect. i.e. The ex. below can be played for *Blackberry Blossom* mm 5-8, *Whiskey Before Breakfast* mm.29-32, and *Dusty Miller* mm. 29-32.
This is a 4-measure pattern which follows a "circular" G scale using a combination of the mini 4-note scale patterns like those presented earlier. In a circular scale, each 4-note group begins with a G major scale tone, playing 3 notes up (or down) the scale, then circling back to the 1st note. The next group begins with the next scale tone, and cycles the same way.
Play only the first note of each group to play the G major scale. G A B G --- **F♯** G A F♯ --- **E** F♯ G E etc. Circular scale patterns may move either up or down the scale line. They also may begin with any note in the scale. Segments may also be used in songs for certain chords, usually beginning with a note belonging to the chord. (Compare this with the pattern in Lesson 10.)
Hints: Notice the left hand *shapes* and look for the familiar *4-note scale patterns* identified earlier.

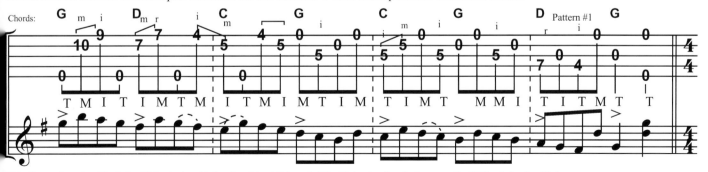

Note: Reverse the order of the 2nd and 3rd notes in m.1 to hear how this might be varied.The 4th 4-note pattern is also reversed in *Whiskey Before Breakfast..*

G Tuning - Key of G
(Optional: Capo 7th fret
to play in Key of D*)
( ) = optional chords

Whiskey Before Breakfast

Slow

Track 55: Fast

The same circular scale pattern may occur in many different songs. Play the last four measures of this arrangement for the last four measures of Part A in *Blackberry Blossom*. The songs sound entirely different due to the different melodies and chord progressions. However, the chords and the function of these 4 measures is the same in both songs. For variety, substitute the circular scale as it currently appears in *Blackberry Blossom* for the last four measures of Part B below.

Try alternate licks for these measures, too. Choose your favorites. This popular fiddle tune can be a lot of fun to play.

Notice how the melody notes work up and down the scale, beginning each new chord with a note belonging to that chord.

Form: Play Part A twice, then Part B twice.

Substitute Licks for Whiskey Before Breakfast:

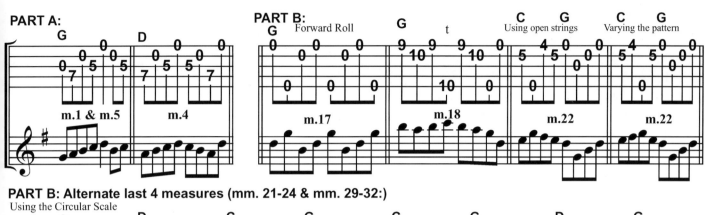

PART B: Alternate last 4 measures (mm. 21-24 & mm. 29-32:)
Using the Circular Scale

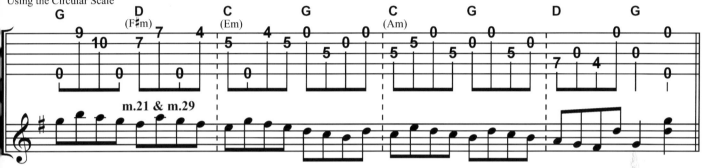

Using the Backward Roll Pattern: (mm. 21-24 & mm. 29-32)

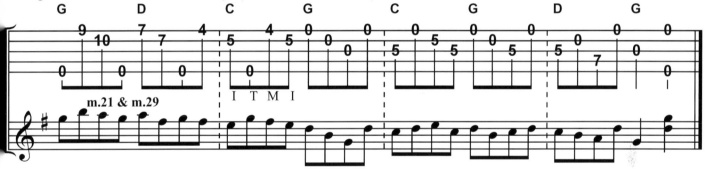

Substituting Triplets:

A triplet may also be played in m.1 and/or in m. 4. In m.1, the 2nd and 3rd notes are played only with the left hand.
The left middle finger hammers on the 2nd fret, then pulls off the string to open.
HINT: Say *"Tri - Po - Let"* as you play the notes in the triplet.

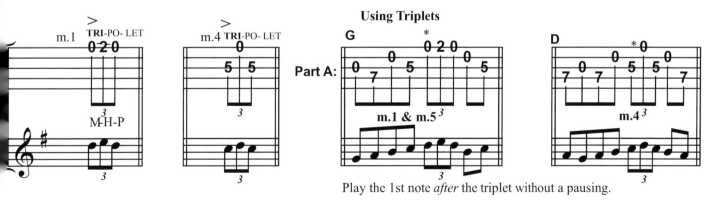

Play the 1st note *after* the triplet without a pausing.

Lesson 14: Melodic Licks by Chord

Demonstrated with Dixie Hoedown

Also: Adding Minor Chords

When a fiddle tune is played in the melodic style virtually every note is a melody note, as a fiddler might play the tune. Where there is a longer note value, the note can be sustained for the duration of that note or "fill" notes can be added, often with an open string to fill the rhythmic space.

Compare the two measures below. The main melody notes for the first measure of *Dixie Hoedown* are provided in the example on the left. Extra fill in notes have been added to the example on the right. This is the first measure in the melodic style arrangement for this tune.

Melody Only for Dixie Hoedown:

Melodic Style with fill in notes:

A "Lick" = 8 notes:

A lick is a picking pattern which is played for a *specific chord(s)*.
Licks are often combinations of the mini 4-note "melodic" scale patterns.
Usually the first note of a lick is a melody note.
A single lick = 1 measure of music usually consisting of 8 notes (eighth notes).

One lick may be used in many different songs for the "assigned" chord. For example, play each of the following 1-measure "C" licks for the C chord in the 2nd measure of *Dixie Hoedown*. They also work for the C chord in the 3rd measure of *Redwing*. Notice how the effect changes when you substitute one for the other.

"C" Melodic Lick (m.19)

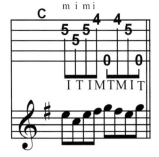

"C" Melodic Lick (m.2)

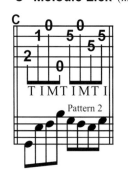

Pattern 2

"D" Lick: (m.22,30)

Also:

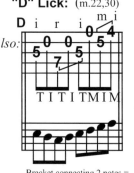

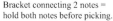

Bracket connecting 2 notes =
hold both notes before picking.

(Part A: m.7)

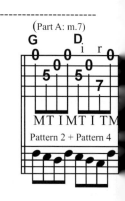

Pattern 2 + Pattern 4

Single licks can also be combined to form 2-measure licks which can be interchanged from song to song by chord. i.e. See the "D" chord in mm.21-22. You may have already noticed that some of the same patterns have been used in multiple songs in this book. i.e. Compare the licks played in *Blackberry Blossom* (mm.5-8) and *Whiskey Before Breakfast* (mm.29-32), which use the same chords. **If you learn these patterns as independent "licks," you can easily incorporate them into other songs for the same chord and function.** The above examples are demonstrated in *Dixie Hoedown*. Isolate these by chord, and try to use them with other songs.

Notes: for the more advanced player:_____

1.) Part A: Measure 16 -- see the alternate measure for this measure under ending 2. This contains triplets which effectively drive the music into Part B. Also, additional licks are provided in this section for substitution in the song.

G Tuning
Key of A: Capo 2nd fret
( ) = optional chord.

Dixie Hoedown

Track 59: Fast
Track 61: Key of A Fast

The intent of this lesson is to provide a fun-to-play melodic style arrangement for a very popular tune using the techniques and patterns discussed so far and to add patterns for minor chords as well as to enhance the awareness of "licks" for specific chords.

Dixie Hoedown has been recorded by Jimmie Lunceford, Don Reno, Jim and Jesse, John Hickman, John McEuen and many other bluegrass musicians and banjo players. Each artist's rendition is slightly different. For example, in Part B the back up chords may be different. The following arrangement includes the minor chords which many players use today. These harmonize with the melody, and although based upon the same scale as the primary major chords, substitute options are common.* i.e. D can be substituted for Bm, and C for Am, and vice versa (except at the very end of the song.) (More in the Notes at the bottom of the following page.)

FORM: Play Part A twice, then Part B twice. When repeating Part A, skip m.8, and substitute m.16.

47

Substitute Licks *for Dixie Hoedown:*

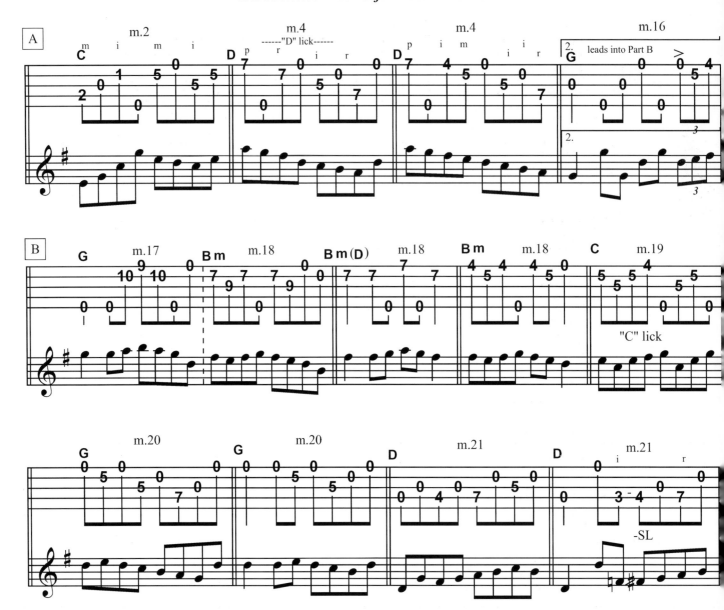

NOTES:_____

In Part B for anyone interested in Chord Theory & Chord & Lick Substitution:

1.) The primary chord, D (V) can be substituted for the Bm (iii) chord and vice versa. Also, the C (IV) can be substituted for the Am (ii). Both chords will work as backup for the same melody notes. All of these notes are from the G major Scale. Notice that the interchangeable chords only differ from each other by one note. The ii chord and the IV chord are often substituted for one another. B7, F♯dim, & F♯m7♭5 have also been substituted for the Bm in Part B.

2.) Watch for the quarter notes (♩) and pause or hold for the duration of an extra eighth note.

Lesson 15: Review - Melodic "Techniques"

Adding an Introduction:

The following is a popular introduction played by the banjo before a fiddle tune begins in the Key of G. Play the same pattern 4 times. The 4th pattern should end with pickup notes for the last beat, to lead into the first measure of the song, i.e. instead of the pinch. (See *Bill Cheatham.*)

-Intro: Play 4 times-

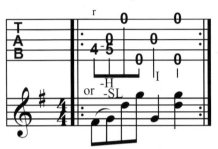

Placing the Melody Notes:

The melody notes are primarily from the G major scale for songs played in the Key of G. The notes which fill in the spaces between the melody notes are either scale tones which connect the melody notes or chord tones of the indicated chord. How the melody notes are combined depends upon the melody note locations and the chords. (See *Bill Cheatham.*) Hint: A melody note is often the first note of the measure. Notice the combined 4-note scale patterns. Accent the first note of each mini scale pattern to bring out the melody notes.

-Melody Notes-

-Melody Melodic Style --with fill in notes from G scale

Triplets:
Play 3 notes in the same amount of time 2 eighth notes are played. A triplet is often used as pickup notes to the open 5th string. Accent the first note of the triplet and the first note following the triplet. (Do not stop after the triplet.).

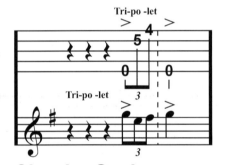

Rhythm Pattern:

This is a commonly used syncopated rhythm using eighth & quarter note combinations. Hold the quarter note the duration of 2 eighth notes.

Short - Long Short - Long

Fretting The 5th String:

The 5th and the 1st string play the identical notes at the same frets. Often, a choice has to be made as to whether to play a note on the 1st string or on the 5th string. The left hand may fret the 5th string with the thumb or a left-hand finger. Whichever is easier usually determines this.

Fret 5th string with Left Thumb

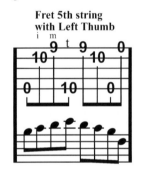

Fret 5th string with Left Ring finger.

Circular Scale:
This scale is built with 4-note scale patterns which move up or down the G scale line. Play 3 notes up (or down the scale) and return to the first note; step up (or down) one note and repeat the sequence. Play only the first of each four-note group; notice this is the G major scale. Many melodic style licks and patterns are derived from the circular scale. See *Whiskey Before Breakfast.*

EXCERCISE: Also, see the Review (Lesson 10) for the descending exercise and combine with the following. Look for the left-hand shapes, too.

Melodic Style "Licks":
Licks are "melodic" patterns for *specific chord(s). Each pattern = 1 measure (8 eighth notes.)*

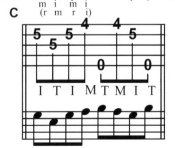

Note: Single licks can also be combined to form 2-measure licks which can be interchanged from song to song by chord.

Lesson 16: Adding The "F" Chord
With The Cuckoo's Nest

The Cuckoo's Nest **includes the** *F chord,* **in addition to using the G, C and D chords,** which are the primary chords in the Key of G and use the standard G scale melodic style fingerboard positions. Instead of playing the F♯, which naturally occurs in the G scale, the F chord plays an F♮ note. This note is always located one fret number lower than the F♯. To quickly find melodic *scale shapes* for the F chord, find the shape(s) used for the D chord --- then simply lower the F♯ note one fret number to the F♮ --- i.e. from the 4th fret to the 3rd fret on the first and fourth strings, from the 7th fret to the 6th fret on the second string, and from the 11th to the 10th of the third string.

⌐──── = hold both notes before picking separately

COMPARING MELODIC SHAPES for the D chord and for the F Chord:

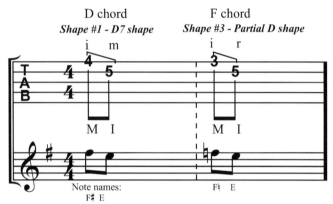

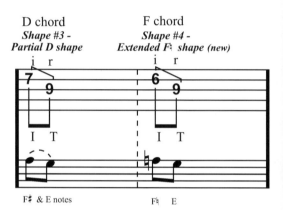

Note: For the "F" chord locations on the fingerboard, see the Alternate Licks for *Cuckoo's Nest*.

Review - PICK UP NOTES with a Triplet:
An effective way to begin a fiddle tune on the banjo is to play a triplet for the pick up notes to add excitement and energy right from the beginning. The following example is very common and can be used to begin any song which starts with the open 5th string in measure 1. i.e. *The Cuckoo's Nest, Blackberry Blossom, Devil's Dream, Fisher's Hornpipe, Big Sandy River,* and more. This may also be used to begin the next phrase within a song. (i.e. *Blackberry Blossom,* m. 4 for the last beat.) And, use these as pickup notes when repeating Part A, (i.e. in *The Cuckoo's Nest,* m.8 for the last beat in the measure.) Note: The triplet may also be played on the same strings as open strings, without fretting them.

> = **Emphasize the 1st note (Tri-po-let).**

Play the note *after* **the triplet without a pause** or break in the rhythm. Emphasize this note, too.

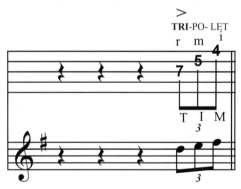

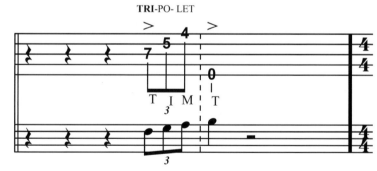

NOTES:_____
1.) The "F" Chord and the "F" note can have several different functions in a song. One is to lead the music to a C chord (see mm. 3-4)
    Another is as a "neighbor chord" which returns to the chord just before it. (i.e. Part B from G to F to G). The "F" chord also can be used
    for a Mixolydian effect, which is derived from the old Church Modes used before Bach established the Major Scale as the Daddy of all Scales
    in American or Western music.
2.) This arrangement for *The Cuckoo's Nest* is played in the Key of G. Musicians also like to play this in the Key of D. These two keys work well
    together, so it is a fairly smooth transition to modulate from one key to the other when playing together. You can also place the capo on the
    7th fret to convert this arrangemet to the Key of D. Near the end of this book is a section on playing in the Key of D also.

G Tuning - Key of G
(Optional: Capo 7th fret for Key of D)

The Cuckoo's Nest

TRACK
3
Slow

Track 4: Fast

This arrangement can tickle your fingers as you play the melody notes up and down the fingerboard of the banjo. Notice that almost every note is an important melody note, which is common for fiddle tunes played in the melodic style. The "F" chord is played for measures 3, 19 and 20. The "F" note is played on the 3rd fret of the 1st & 4th strings, instead of on the 4th fret which is an F♯. (This changes the left-hand shape to the Partial D shape.)

Notice the rhythm as well: Each quarter note should be held for the same amount of time it takes to play two eighth notes: ♩ = ♪♪

Play Part A twice, then Part B twice. Substitute the 2nd ending (m.16) for the 1st ending, (m.8) when repeating Part A, and m.32 for m.24 when repeating Part B.

51

Substitute Licks
for The Cuckoo's Nest

Optional Ending:

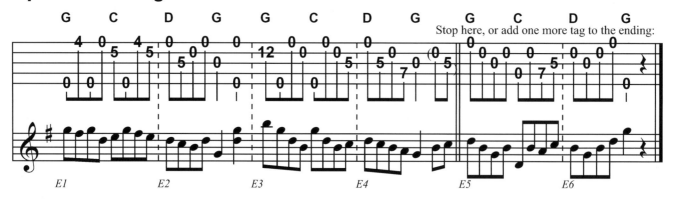

Substitute Licks:

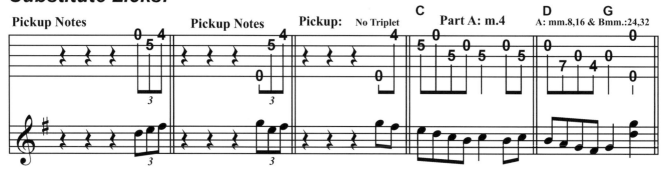

All "F" Chord Locations on the Fingerboard:

The "F" melodic shapes are *partial* F chord shapes, usually played on two adjacent strings.

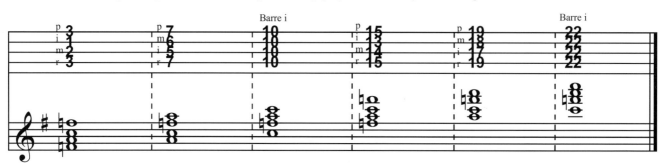

Note: See Lessons 22 & 23 for more about chords and full chord positions.

Lesson 17: "F" Shapes & Mixolydian

With Dusty Miller Hornpipe

⌐─┐ = Hold both notes but pick separately

The Key of G "Mixolydian": Primary Chords = G & F

The *Dusty Miller Hornpipe* is an example of a song which uses the G and F chords as the primary chords. This type of chord combination draws from a G scale which plays an F♮ instead of an F♯. This is called the (G) Mixolydian Mode. The "F" Chord involves holding additional left hand *shapes*. Compare the following to the shapes presented in the earlier lessons and notice these are similar shapes, but instead of playing the 4th fret on the 1st string or 4th string, (F♯), the F chord plays the 3rd fret (F♮). In the following examples, the F♯ has been lowered one fret number to an F.

Melodic SHAPES using the F natural note:

Scale Shapes for F and E notes
Bracket = hold both notes before picking

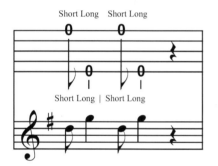

New **Chord Shapes** which include the "F" chord tones on 2 strings

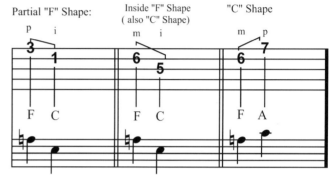

RHYTHM (Review): The rhyhm in measure 20 of Part B should be recognizable by now. This popular syncopated rhythm is used in many fiddle and banjo tunes: ♪ ♩ = short - long   ie. Also see *Whiskey Before Breakfast & Big Scioty* (part B.)

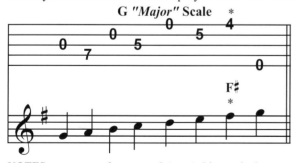

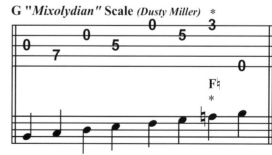

COMPARING the "G" MAJOR Scale with the "G" MIXOLYDIAN Scale:

Only one note is different!

The G Major Scale and the G Mixolydian Scale use the same notes, except for the 7th note.

As mentioned above, *Dusty Miller* uses the G and F chords as the primary chords. When these two chords are the main chords for a song, it is a signal that the melody and chords will use the Mixolydian Scale ("mode").

The G Major Scale and the G Mixolydian Scale use the same notes, except for the 7th note. This note is played one fret lower for the mixolydian mode. Essentially, this tells you to play an F♮ instead of an F♯. Flat the 7th note of the major scale (F) for the mixolydian mode. The G scale plays F♯ and the G mixolydian plays F♮.

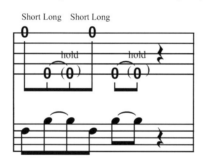

NOTES_____for anyone interested in music theory:

1.) The **G** *Mixolydian* Scale uses the same tones in the **C** Major Scale, but is played from G to G.
   Mixolydian means it starts and ends with the 5th note of a major scale. The letter name of the *Mixolydian* Scale is 5 letters up the alphabet from the root of the Major Scale. C -- to G = 5 letters. When compared with the Major Scale with the same name, only the 7th tone is altered. It is flatted, (played 1 fret lower) in the *Mixolydian* mode.

Dusty Miller Hornpipe

Look at the chords in the arrangement below and notice that the G and F chords are the primary chords.
As discussed on the previous page, this type of chord sequence draws from a scale called the *Mixolydian Mode. The primary chords are **G** and **F** when a song is built with the Mixolydian scale tones, instead of G and D. The F chord is usually used instead of the D chord, when a song is played in the G mixolydian mode. **Today, people often play the D chord just before the final G chord as they are used to hearing this in traditional music.** (If you substitute the F chord for the D chord, you may find the song will still sound fine.) Also, look through the arrangement to identify the F chord shapes for the left-hand shape.
It is important to realize that this one note creates an entirely different effect. **Learn to identify this modal "sound," as you will discover many songs which use the Mixolydian mode (G & F chords).**

FORM: Part A twice; **Part B** twice; **Part C** twice. (Repeat each section before continuing.)

****Notice that Part B, mm. 21-24 plays the circular scale** also used in *Blackberry Blossom* and *Whiskey Before Breakfast*.*

(like *Blackberry Blossom & Whiskey Before Breakfast*)

Notes:_____

1.) The key signature for *Dusty Miller Hornpipe* is the Key of G major and includes the F♯. Each F♮ note will include the natural sign in the music.

2.) The hornpipe is played at a bouncy, brisk tempo, slightly slower than a reel. The original hornpipes date back to the 16th century. The name for the tune is also often shortened, omitting the word" Hornpipe" in the title.

Dusty Miller Hornpipe continued

Part C: (Variation of Part A)

Track 8: Fast

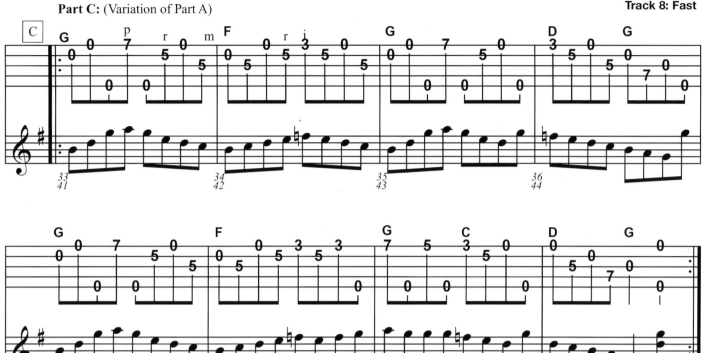

Substitute Licks:

Part A:

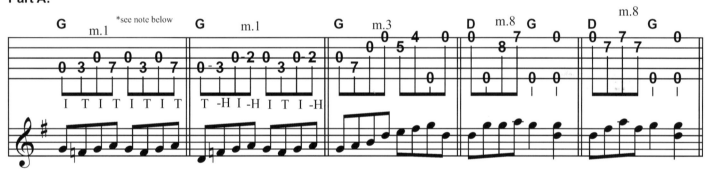

Part B:

Part C:

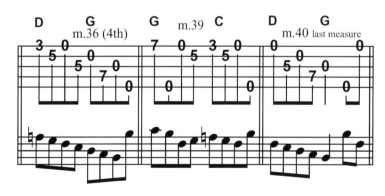

NOTES:_____

1.) (i.e. In m.1) When 2 notes are played in a row on the same string, the left-hand hammer (or pull off or slide) is also effective in the melodic style.
   It is also fine to pick each note using the single-string picking techqnique by altering the thumb & index fingers of the right hand.

Lesson 18: Using The Capo
Also: Playing Scale Pattern #1 for the "F" Chord
With Red Haired Boy

Many fiddle tunes are traditionally played in a "specific" key. The Key of A is popular among fiddle and mandolin players. *Cripple Creek* is an example of a tune normally played in the Key of A. *Fire on the Mountain* and *Red Haired Boy* are also played in the Key of A. In a jam session or when performing these tunes, the audience and other musicians will expect to hear the banjo playing the tune in the appropriate key. With the capo on the 2nd fret, the G scale tones will be raised to those belonging to the A scale. Play the song exactly the same way, as if you are in the key of G, but the notes will actually be in the Key of A. When you pick the open 3rd string with the capo on the 2nd fret, your banjo is playing an A note instead of a G note.

On the banjo in the melodic style, it is easiest to learn the song without the capo, in the open G tuning. Once you know the song, place the capo across the 2nd fret (or the designated fret for that specific song). Play the song exactly as you play it without the capo; the capo now becomes the string nut. This shortens the neck and raises the pitch of each note two frets higher (one whole step). Play the song with the capo from then on, and it will sound right. Also, it may be easier to play.

CHANGING THE KEY TO "A" with a capo at the 2nd fret:

1.) Play the G scale without the capo. 2.) Then, place the capo on the 2nd fret and play the same notes.
The capo simply shortens the neck. ***Remember to adjust your 5th string up 2 frets also.
With your capo on the 2nd fret, this scale becomes the A scale as it is playing the pitches which belong to the A scale.
The pitch is higher with the capo on the 2nd fret, without having to change the positions of your left-hand fingers.
On the 2nd fret, the capo causes a song in the Key of G to automatically be played in the Key of A.

The "G" Major Scale: (sounds like "A" scale w/capo at 2nd fret)

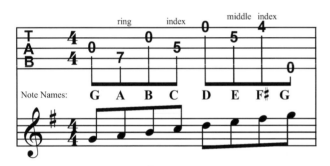

The "A" Scale played without a capo:

COMPARING "*SCALE PATTERN #1*" for the "D" Chord and for the "F" Chord:

Scale Pattern #1 was discussed with *Fire on the Mountain* as a common set of 4 notes from the G scale, often used for the D chord in the Key of G. To play this pattern for the F chord, simply lower the note on the 4th string/4th fret (F♯) to the 3rd fret (F♮). By simply moving one note down one fret, this pattern can now be played for the F Chord.
Red Haired Boy includes the following scale pattern for the F chord in Part A, m.4, and in Part B, m.20.

Scale Pattern #1

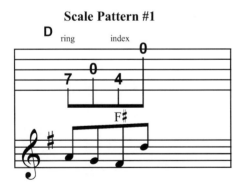

Scale Pattern #1-F

NOTES for those interested in Music Theory:_____

1.) *In Red Haired Boy*, the usual F♯ in the fourth measure on the 4th string/4th fret, is lowered to an F natural (4th string/3rd fret.) The Mixolydian G scale is like the G major scale, but played with an F natural instead of an F♯. It uses the tones of the C scale, but is played from G to G. Many traditional fiddle tunes and bluegrass tunes (*i.e. Dusty Miller Hornpipe, Red Haired Boy, Old Joe Clark, Wheel Hoss, Little Maggie, etc.*) are based upon the Mixolydian mode, using the G and F chords as the primary chords. (See *Dusty Miller Hornpipe* for more on the Mixolydian scale.)

G Tuning - G Mixolydian
Capo 2nd Fret - Key of A Mixolydian:

Red Haired Boy

Before you play through *Red Haired Boy*, look for the now familiar left-hand shapes and how the melody works up and down the scale line. Also, look for repetitions. For example, mm. 4-8 in Part A are exactly the same as the last 4 measures of Part B. Once you have learned this tune, place your capo on the 2nd fret every time you play it, especially when you perform this song for others as it is traditionally played in the Key of A. Note: Remember to compensate the 5th string the same distance (2 frets higher).

FORM: Play Part A (mm.1-8) two times, then play Part B two times.

Note: See *Old Joe Clark* (the last song in this book) for an arrangement in the Key of A without using the capo.

57

Lesson 19: Adding "Chromatic" Notes
Demonstrated with Old Joe Clark

Chromatic tones are often used in the melodic style as a "fill" between two melody notes. A *chromatic** tone occurs *between* two melody notes of the major scale line. These notes are effective for adding interest and/or energy to a passage. A chromatic note may be used as a passing tone to connect the two melody notes, or as a neighboring tone which returns to the same melody note, as in m.1 of *Old Joe Clark*.

As a passing tone:

Note names: C   C♯   D

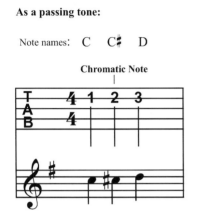

As a neighbor tone:

D   C♯   D

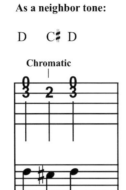

Measure 1 in *Old Joe Clark* - melodic style

D C♯ D

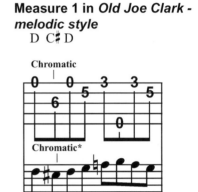

Comparing the "G" Major Scale with the "G" Chromatic Scale on one string:

A *"major scale"* includes seven notes which repeat up the fingerboard. This scale follows a fretboard pattern when played up the same string which can be learned like a phone number. The major scale can begin with any note, as long as the other notes are found using this pattern: 2 2 1 - 2 2 2 1. A *"chromatic" scale* consists of 12 notes which repeat as you go up the fingerboard. This scale plays a note on *every fret* when played up the same string. 1 1 1 1 1 1 etc.

G Major Scale = 7 Notes:

The G major Scale uses a fretboard pattern up one string, starting with the note named for the scale.

+ 2 frets +2 frets +1 fret + 2 +2 +2 +1

G Chromatic Scale = 12 Notes:

The chromatic scale includes *every fret along one string.* It consists of 12 tones starting with the note named for the scale. i.e. G chromatic scales starts with G note. One fret = 1/2 step in music theory; two frets - 1 whole step.

NOTES:_____
1.) When a chromatic note is placed between two melody notes, it can function in two different ways:
   a.) Neighbor Tone - the *same* melody note is on each side of the chromatic note (See ex. 1 above).
   b.) Passing Tone - the chromatic tone is between two different melody notes in the scale, and is used to connect them.
2.) Technically, the 3rd fret (F natural) on the first string is also a chromatic tone when compared with the G major scale.
   "Old Joe Clark" however, uses the G Mixolydian Scale with the F natural. Therefore, the F natural is actually a melody note.
3.) See *Big Scioty* for another tune which uses chromatic tones as part of the effect.

Standard G Tuning
Key of A: Capo 2nd Fret
( ) = optional note or chord

Old Joe Clark

Track 15 Slow
Track 16: Fast

Old Joe Clark is a well-known song among banjo players of all playing levels. The melodic style version below is also effective when contrasted with a standard bluegrass version in a performance. The *chromatic notes* are indicated above the tab, as well as the now familiar *scale patterns* by number. Notice also that the 1st string, 3rd fret is played instead of the usual 1st string, 4th fret from the G major scale line. In other words, the melody line uses an F instead of an F♯. Like *Dusty Miller Hornpipe, Old Joe Clark* was originally composed in "G" Mixolydian, with the primary chords of G & F. Today, musicians often play a D chord at the end of each section to give the song the usual V-I (D-G) sound they are used to hearing in modern times. For an old-time sound, play the F chord instead of the D chord. The backup chords may be played as indicated (which are fairly standard for this tune) or with the optional chords in parenthesis. The D and F chords are interchangeable. See *Bill Cheatham* for an intro.

Form: = Play Part A twice, then play Part B twice.

NOTES:_____
1.) The above arrangement should be played with the capo on the 2nd fret. See the end of this book in the section on playing in other keys without the capo for an arrangement in the Key of A without using the capo.
2.) *See the end of this book for an arrangement of *Old Joe Clark* in the Key of A without using the capo and without retuning.

Lesson 20: The Old Timey Sound Melodic Style

> = emphasize this note
With Big Scioty

People often wonder why a particular song has a certain "sound." This lesson incorporates several melodic style techniques in order to acheive an old timey effect in *Big Scioty*, which is a popular traditional tune among old time and 3-finger style players. Each of the following contributes to this overall old-time effect.

1.) TRIPLET PICK UP NOTES with DOUBLE HAMMER:

The pickup notes for *Big Scioty* use a double hammer for the 2nd and 3rd notes to play the *triplet*. This is a popular left-hand technique in "old time" clawhammer banjo playing and is effective to use at the beginning of a song in the melodic style for this effect. Pick the open 4th string with the right thumb, then hammer twice in a row with the left-hand fingers without picking the strings with the right hand to play the next two notes of the triplet. *Accent the "tri-."* Do not pause after the triplet - immediately play the first note of m. 1. (See Lesson 12 for standard Melodic Style Triplets.)

2.) SPECIAL PICKING TECHNIQUES to include an individual melody note smoothly:

a.) Picking the Inside Strings with the Right Middle Finger:

See m. 3 in *Big Scioty*. This was also demonstrated in Lesson 11 with *Bill Cheatham* and appears in the alternate licks for *Fire on the Mountain*. where a melody note occurs on an inside string. (*The second half of this measure is a variation of Scale Pattern #1. The P stands for Pentatonic.*)

b.) Fretting the 5th String:

Big Scioty: Part B- mm18,19.
See *Lesson 13 (in Whiskey Before Breakfast.)*

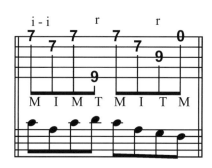

3.) BASIC MELODY NOTES for *Big Scioty:*

Often the scale choice upon which a tune is based provides a natural type of overall effect. The melody for *Big Scioty* uses a (5 note) "Pentatonic" G scale: G A B D E. This seems like a fancy term but is actually a very simple scale. *The melody uses only 5 tones from the standard G major scale.* Compare the G Pentatonic scale notes with the G major scale. The melodic style works with these scale notes using the same techniques used for melodies from the major scale. With practice, the sound of the pentatonic scale in a melody is identifiable. This scale is prevalent in many old time fiddle & banjo tunes.

"G" Major Scale
Melodic Style - 7 notes

Note Names: G A B C D E F♯ G

"G" Pentatonic Scale
Melodic Style - 5 notes

Note Names: G A B D E G

Notes:
1.) The G Pentatonic Scale omits the C and the F♯ (4th & 7th notes) from the standard G major scale. It only uses 5 notes from the G Scale: G,A,B,D,E.
2.) CHROMATIC NOTES also contribute to the effect in *Big Scioty*. These occur *right at the beginning in* measure 1.
   (See Lesson 19 for more on chromatic notes.)

Big Scioty

G Tuning - Key of G
( ) = optional

Track 18 Slow
Track 19: Fast

The following version includes many familiar melodic style patterns. The placement of the melody notes within these patterns contributes to the old time effect. **Measure 3 should be a familiar pattern** by now, and brings the right middle finger inside to the 2nd string. This is a popular pattern for the G and the D chords in the melodic style. **The melody for *Big Scioty* is based upon the 5-note G pentatonic scale.** The notes which fill in the spaces between the melody notes are also, for the most part, from the same set of notes. **However, in measure 1, neighboring chromatic tones are included which add color & motion.***
(See the notes at the bottom of the page.)

Note: The chords indicated include optional choices. Because this is an old tune, it has also been played effectively with the chords in the ( ) parenthesis, also. If choosing the chords in ( ), use only these choices. The C and the Em have been interchanged with one another. Notice how different the effect is which comparing these. **Form: Play A twice, then B twice.**

NOTES: _____

1.) Compare the melody notes in this arrangement to the notes in the pentatonic scale on the previous page. Also, notice the notes between the melody notes. When a note from the G major scale is inserted between 2 melody notes, it is a "passing tone" or a "neighbor" tone.
 The 2nd note in m. 1 is a neighbor tone, because the 3rd note returns to the same melody note.
 Notes from the chromatic scale may also be included (chromatic scale is played on every fret up one string.)
Passing Tone: A scale tone which connects 2 *different* melody notes, adding motion and filling the holes.
Neighboring Tone: A scale tone played between two notes with the same pitch.
Chromatic Tone: Occurs between two notes of the major scale line, m.1 6th note = chromatic neighbor tone. (Also, see *Bill Cheatham,* Alt. Licks.)

For fun, substitute the alternate licks in the previous arrangement. Compare these with the same measure(s) in the arrangement to see how each one can affect the sound and playability.

Part A:

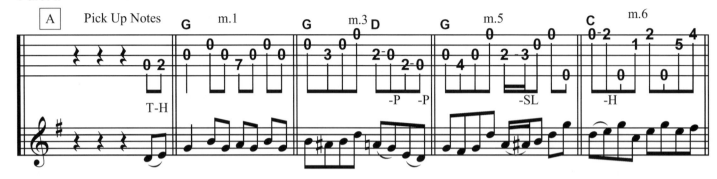

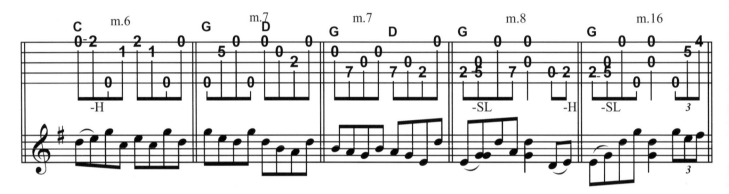

Part B:

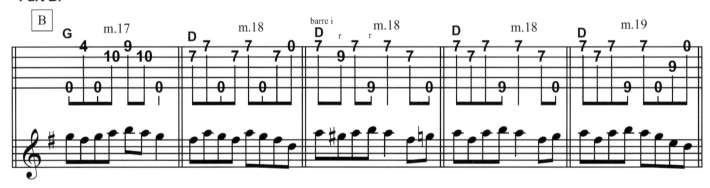

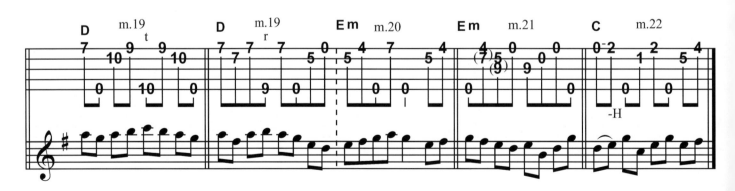

Lesson 21: Review -"F" Chord & Modal & Chromatic Scales

An easy way to find the melodic left-hand shapes played for the F chord is to first locate the shapes played for the D chord - then lower the F♯ note one fret to F♮. (See Lesson 16 with *The Cuckoo's Nest.*)

COMPARING MELODIC *SCALE* SHAPES:
The D CHORD Shapes and the F CHORD Shapes

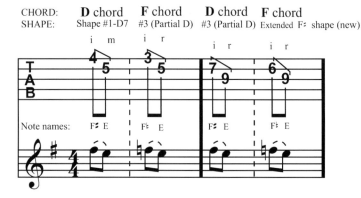

L.H. SHAPES for the "F" chord tones:
These are partial "F" chords.
See *The Cuckoo's Nest, Dusty Miller, Old Joe Clark*

F chords:

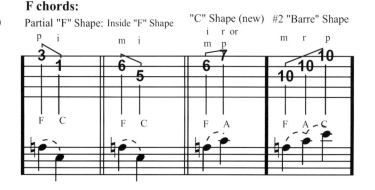

COMPARING the "G" MAJOR Scale and "G" MIXOLYDIAN Scale:

Many of the old mountain tunes from Appalachia use the G and F chords as the primary chords for the backup, instead of the usual G, C and D chords which are drawn from the G major scale. These songs are "modal." When a song's primary chords are G & F, the scale from which the song draws the melody is the G Mixolydian Scale. The G Major Scale and the G Mixolydian Scale use the same notes, except for the 7th note. **Only one note is different!** (See Lesson 17 w/ *Dusty Miller.*)

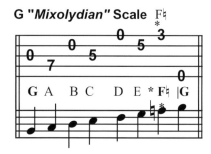

"F" Chord Locations:
All of these are chord tones in the F chord.* The G chord is played 2 frets higher than each F chord location using the same left hand shape.

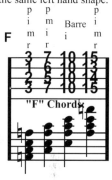

"CHROMATIC" Notes:
A *chromatic** tone occurs between two notes of the major scale line. Chromatic tones are often used in the melodic style as a "fill" between two melody notes. See Lesson 19 w/ *Old Joe Clark* & Lesson 20 w/ *Big Scioty.*

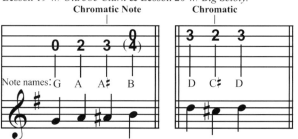

The 'G' *Chromatic* Scale along one string
includes every fret from 0 to 12.

The Major Scale Note Names are Bolded - Chromatic Names are marked.

EXERCISE: The Chromatic Scale played in 3-finger Melodic Style:

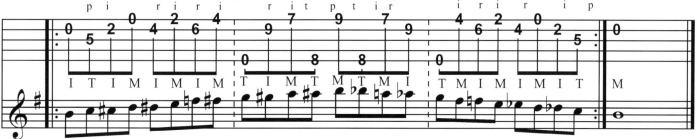

NOTE: You can also substitute your right thumb for the index on the second string where possible in the last half or m.1.

NOTE:_____The chords for each song are indicated above the staff. The left-hand shapes and scale patterns containing the melody notes are played for these chords.

Lesson 22: The Major Chord Shapes

Demonstrated with Sailor's Hornpipe

One way to move up the neck is working up the scale line. Another is to connect the tones which belong to a chord by moving to the next position of the same chord or a different chord. In the beginning of this book, three left-hand *scale shapes* were presented. Each 2-note shape was numbered and named according to a chord or partial chord shape. Full chords are also used in the melodic style with the left hand. There are also only three left-hand shapes for holding the full chord positions for any chord. (Pick any two adjacent strings in each chord shape to see how the scale shapes are drawn from these chord positions.)

Every major chord can be played by holding the same left hand *"chord shape."* As the left hand moves the chord shape up one fret at a time, the chord being played changes names alphabetically as well as in pitch. The same chord (i.e. the G chord), can be played with each of the three chord shapes.* *The "Barre" Shape, the "F" Shape and the "D" Shape. (The latter two are named for the lowest chord that may be played with that shape.)*

EACH CHORD "SHAPE" appears below showing the locations for every MAJOR CHORD on the fingerboard: **Learn the locations for the G, C, and D chords using each shape.** Note: *Any* other chord can be found in relation to these. The G scale notes are played along the 3rd string string: **F is designated instead of F♯, in order to locate the F chords.** (F♯ is one fret higher.) i.e. the F chord is 2 frets below G when holding the same shape with the left hand; the A chord is always played 2 frets higher than G.
Note: The "root" of the chord is the note which has the same name as the chord.

THE THREE CHORD S*HAPES:*

NOTE: The note on the 4th string is on the same fret # as the 1st string for each chord.
NOTE: Hold the shape at the indicated fret number (highest number in the shape) to find any chord.
*NOTE: In the "Barre" Shape, the "root" of the chord is played on the 3rd string.

"BARRE" SHAPE:
Barre one left finger across all of the strings:

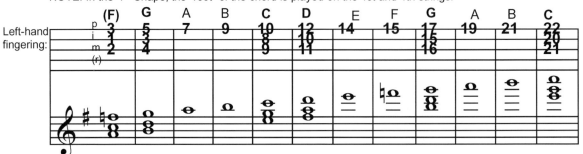

*NOTE: In the "F" Shape, the "root" of the chord is played on the 1st and 4th strings.

"F" SHAPE: Left-hand fingering:

*NOTE: In the "D" Shape, the "root" of the chord is played on the 2nd string.

"D" SHAPE
Like the F shape, but the fingers on the 2 inside strings change places. The D shape is played 4 frets higher than the F shape for the same chord.

Notes:
1.) Play each shape up the fingerboard to hear each chord that can be played with that shape.
2.) F♯ is played one fret higher than F natural. With the F instead of the F♯, the G scale uses the mixolydian mode, mentioned in the section on playing the F chord in the Key of G. The F chord is much more likely to occur in songs based around the Key of G than the F♯ major chord.
3.) The "ROOT" of the chord is the note named for the chord. i.e. G is the root note of the G chord, C is the root note of the C chord.

The next lesson will connect the notes in the same chord as you move from shape to shape up the neck.

Standard G tuning: Key of G
Capo 2nd fret for Key of A

Sailor's Hornpipe

TRACK **23**
Slow

Track 24: Fast
Track 27: Key of A Fast

Sailor's Hornpipe **is a happy sounding, recognizable favorite among audiences.** Bill Keith recorded this tune with Bill Monroe, in the early 1960s, playing it in the new melodic or fiddle style on the banjo. This tune has become a banjo classic.

Chords: The "A" major (m.3) chord and "D" major (m.4) chord are played in the "F" shape locations for these 2 chords.

Rhythm: When playing through this, pause for each quarter note to keep the correct timing.
Each quarter note is held for the duration of 2 eighth notes: ♩ = ♪ ♪

Form: Play Part A through m.8; return to m.1 and repeat Part A. Skip Ending 1 (m. 8) and substitute Ending 2 (m.16).
Then continue with Part B which is also played twice.

Substitute Licks: *for Sailor's Hornpipe*

The above ending is inspired by Daddy Dave Wood's ending for this tune.

Lesson 23: *The Major Chord Locations* Up The Neck
Demonstrated with Twinkle Little Star

TRACK 28

In the following song, chords are part of the charm of the song. Notice how they provide a rhythmic and melodic relief from the tension of the melodic scale patterns. When chords are held in the melodic style, it is not uncommon to move from one shape to another of the same chord. This smoothly moves the music into another area of the fingerboard while also connecting the melody notes musically. i.e. see m.3 in *Twinkle Little Star.* A song may also play different chords in the same area of the fingerboard as in Part B, m.19.

It is helpful to learn the locations of the primary chords in a song in advance, as the left hand will automatically use the proper fingering as they occur. And, of course, these chords recur in many different songs.

REVIEW: Only three left-hand shapes are used to play each major chord.

Note: Each shape is named for the lowest chord played using that shape. i.e. F shape is named for the F chord.
NOTE: The note on the 4th string is on the same fret number as the note on the 1st string for each chord shape.
NOTE: The fingerboard repeats at the 12th fret. Think of the 12th fret as the string nut to locate the chords i.e. 12 + 5= C chord.

USING THE SAME SHAPE: The locations for all of the G, C, and D CHORDS

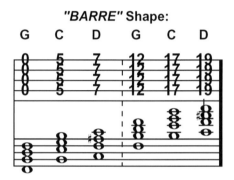

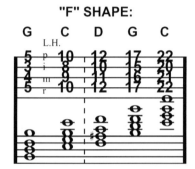

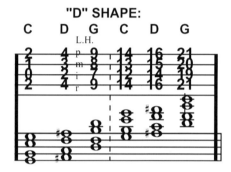

ALL LOCATIONS for ONE CHORD using the three left-hand shapes.

As the left hand moves from one location to the next, the shape changes in a sequence. Notice that the *F shape* goes up to the *D shape* which goes up to the *Barre Shape* for each chord. Also notice that the note on the top (1st) string moves over to the next string when moving to the next location. In the F shape, the "root" of the chord is on the 1st string (& 4th string), the root moves to the 2nd string in the D shape, and to the 3rd string in the Barre Shape.
(The root [G] is the note named for the chord [G chord].)
NOTE: See the previous lesson for the locations of all of the major chords commonly used in the Key of G.

TRACK 29

All "G" Chord Locations:

All "C" Chord Locations:

All "D" Chord Locations: The "D" chord is always located 2 frets higher than the C chord with the same shape.

Additional Major Chords often used in the Key of G:

"A" Chord Locations: The "A" chord is always located 2 frets higher than the G chord with the same shape.

"B" Chord Locations: The "B" chord is always located 4 frets higher than the G chord with the same shape, (and 1 fret lower than the C chord with the same shape).

"E" Chord Locations: The "E" chord is always located 2 frets higher than the D chord with the same shape.

"F" Chord Locations: The "F" chord is always located 2 frets lower than the G chord with the same shape.

NOTE: The A minor and B minor chord positions are played as substitute chords for the D chord and the C chord in Part B of *Twinkle Little Star*, mm. 20. To form the substituted minor chord, notice that only one note is changed from the major chord.

TRACK
30
Slow
Track 31: Fast

G Tuning: Key of G
( ) = optional

Twinkle Little Star *(fiddle tune)*

Twinkle Little Star is a popular fiddle tune and is quite different from the alphabet melody with the two
"twinkles" in Lesson 8. This arrangement is fun to play and uses a combination of many, if not most of the
techniques covered so far. Before playing through this, look for the following:

1.) Up The Neck: The melody for this tune goes futher up the scale line than the previous tunes.

2.) Scale Shapes: *Look for the familiar "scale" shapes.* Rhythmically, the scale shapes may also cross over the bar line between
two measures. In m.1, the last note forms the "Partial D" shape with the first note of m.2.

3.) Chords: In Part B, the left hand holds chord shapes while the right hand picks the three notes in each chord.
This passage is an "identifiable element unique to *Twinkle Little Star.* The minor chords in parenthesis are substitute chords for
the primary major chords (G, C and D).

4.) Chromatic tones (notes between the scale tones) are also used, as in m.7 for the A chord, and the first measure of Part B.

5.) Look for "Licks" by chord which can be used in other songs for the same chord.
i.e m.7 can be used for the A chord in other songs which lead to the D chord on the open 1st string.

FORM : Play Part A once (16 mm.); Play Part B once (16 mm.) There are no repeated parts in this arrangement.

( ) = optional

Twinkle Little Star Continued

Note: See the alternate licks for Part B if this section is difficult for you. These also sound fine and are easier to play.

Notes:_____

1.) The above arrangement uses many more of the techniques discussed in this book than were mentioned in the introduction to this song. Look for the triplets, using the thumb on the 5th string, playing the F natural shapes as well as the standard left-hand shapes, and more!

Substitute Licks for Twinkle Little Star:

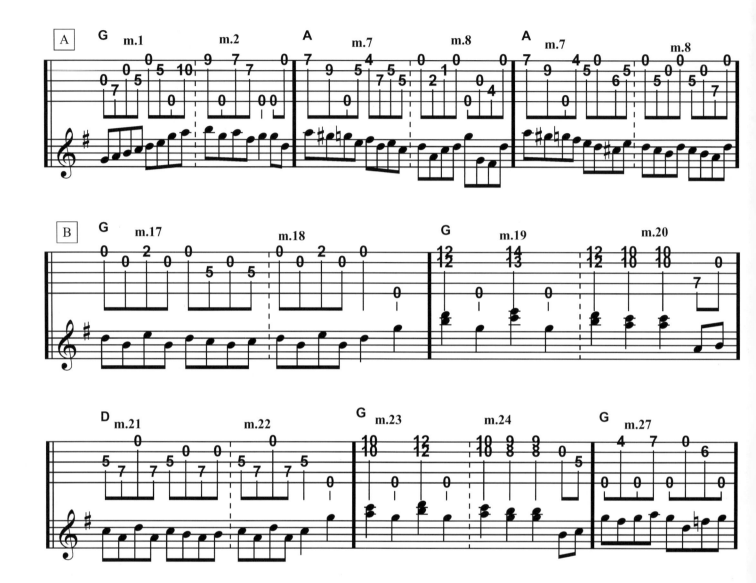

Note: The bar line beween two measures with dashes separating them = substitute both measures to be played together.

Lesson 24: Contrasting Bluegrass & the Melodic Style
Demonstrated with Sally Goodin'

This lesson is concerned with how to convert a bluegrass arrangement of bluegrass rolls and licks to a melodic style arrangement. Often, a song will begin with one style, then for a second variation, contrast may be added with the melodic style or vice versa. *Sally Goodin'* is commonly played in either style, so it is handy to know a version in each style. Notice the sound of the chord tones for harmony in the bluegrass style as opposed to the scale tones in the melodic style.

In the melodic arrangement, *Sally Goodin'* is based primarily upon the left-hand D7 Shape, as is *Cripple Creek* in Lesson 1, and *Katy Hill* in Lesson 25.

1.) Bluegrass with Rolls and Chords -

Sally Goodin': **Part A:** For example, measures 1 & 2:
Hold the Em chord with the left hand and use the left pinky for the notes on the second string. (The backup chord is a G chord.)

2.) Melodic Style with Left-Hand Scale Shape #1 -The "D7" Shape
as primary with the left hand throughout *Sally Goodin'*. Find the main melody notes with the left-hand shapes so that scale tones provide the background notes instead of chord tones. The right-hand patterns are similar, but altered to fit the scale line.

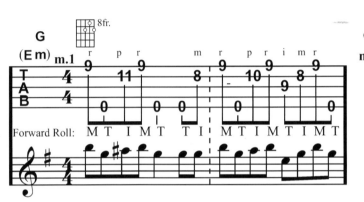

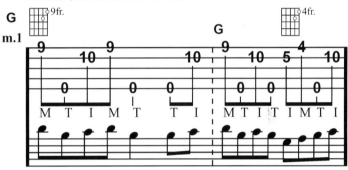

3.) Compare Sally Goodin' below in the bluegrass style with the melodic arrangement on the following page.

Sally Goodin' - Bluegrass Style

Track 34 Slow

Track 35: Fast

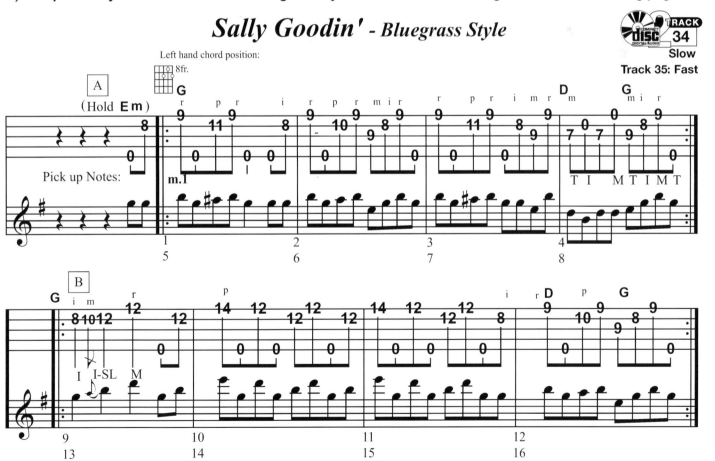

71

Key of G
Capo 2nd fret for Key of A

Sally Goodin'

- Melodic Style Arrangement -

Track 37: Fast

The following arrangement is a melodic style arrangement for *Sally Goodin'*, which uses the left-hand melodic D7 shape throughout. Compare this arrangement with the bluegrass style arrangement on the previous page to see how the scale tones are used instead of chord tones. Also, compare this arrangement with the arrangement in Lesson 1 for *Cripple Creek* and with *Katy Hill* in Lesson 24. The *melodic "D7 shape"* is dominant with the left hand for each of these songs, yet the songs are entirely different. The melody notes are supported by scale tones in the same locations, but at different times. Because all of the songs are played in the key of G, they all work along the G scale line using the G scale tones for the melody as well as the background note. In the melodic style, the scale tones played between the melody notes add drive and a sense of direction and connection with the melody notes.

FORM: Play Part A twice, then play Part B twice. The opening notes are optional pick up notes, which can be played or omitted.

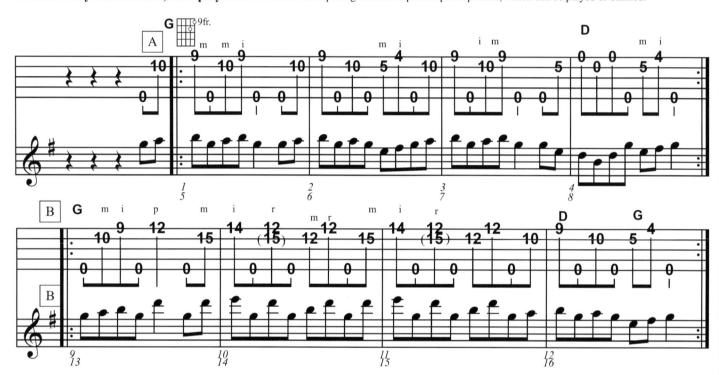

Substitute Licks in the Melodic Style for Sally Goodin'

Part A:

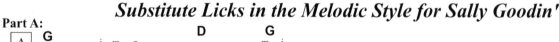

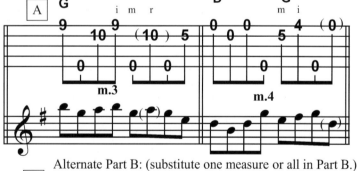

Alternate Part B: (substitute one measure or all in Part B.)

Lesson 25: Combining Bluegrass & the Melodic Style
Demonstrated with Katy Hill

TRACK 39

This lesson demonstrates one way the melodic style and traditional bluegrass rolls and licks can work together in the same arrangement for a song. It is often effective to include bluegrass rolls and licks in a melodic style arrangement. In *Katy Hill*, Part A is played in the melodic style while Part B is played with traditional bluegrass licks. Before playing through the song, compare *Katy Hill* with *Cripple Creek* (the first lesson in this course). There are many surprising similarities, especially in the left-hand patterns, even though the songs sound entirely different. Part B of *Cripple Creek* could also be varied with the standard bluegrass rolls and licks.

1.) SHAPES: Part A - Shape #1 - "D7"
Melodic Shape is dominant with the left hand throughout Part A of *Katy Hill*.

Part A: For example: measures 2 & 3:

2.) A "MELODIC" LICK is played for the
last two measures of Part A & Part B.

This pattern can be (and is) used in many different songs and is effective when improvising over these specific chords.

This 2-measure "lick" is formed by combining two 1-measure licks.

Lick (2 measures) (See *Blackberry Blossom*, Lesson 2 also.)

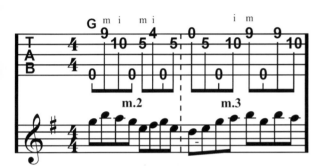

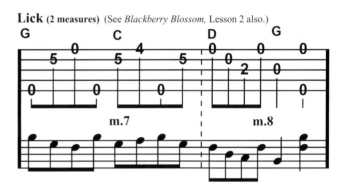

3.) PART B is played in a traditional bluegrass fashion, except for the closing melodic licks in the last 2 measures.
Compare these measures with Part B of *Cripple Creek,* in Lesson 1, especially the chords and duration of each chord. Part B of *Katy Hill* can also be substituted for Part B of *Cripple Creek,* with only slight changes to give it a bluegrass flavor. In *Cripple Creek*, m.20 should be the *open* third string (for the G chord instead of D chord). Compare the following two examples. One is used in *Katy Hill* and the other could be played for Part B of *Cripple Creek*.
Notice that each measure uses the Mixed (Alt. Thumb) Roll Pattern with the right hand (TITM TITM.).

Katy Hill measures 19 & 20:

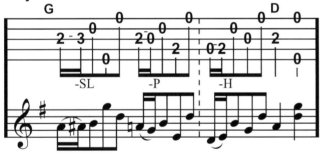

Substitute in *Cripple Creek* for mm 19 & 20:

4.) "G" PENTATONIC Scale: This is a five-note scale: G A B D E. Notice this scale is like the G major scale,
but omits the 4th and 7th notes. This five-note scale is the basis for the melody for many fiddle and bluegrass tunes. In *Katy Hill*, this scale provides the main melody notes. Other notes included are used as passing tones, rather than primary melody notes.

G Pentatonic Scale Notes:

On ONE STRING::

Melodic Style

All locations from open to 12th fret

Key of G: G Tuning
G Pentatonic Scale:
5 notes: G A B D E

Lesson 25: Combining Melodic Style with Bluegrass

Track 40 Slow
Track 41: Fast

Katy Hill

Part A is played in the melodic style while Part B is played in the traditional bluegrass style.

Katy Hill is a popular fiddle tune among banjo players and is not difficult to play, even though it may sound difficult. The following arrangement demonstrates how the melodic style and the bluegrass style rolls and licks can be used in a single arrangement for a fiddle tune. **FORM: Play Part A twice, then play Part B twice.**

PART A: Shape #1, the D7 Shape is dominant throughout, as it was in *Cripple Creek* (the first song in this book).

PART B: uses many of the traditional bluegrass techniques involving roll patterns and left-hand slides, pull offs and hammers.

NOTE: Notice there are no pick up notes. The opening notes feel like pick up notes, but actually occur as the first notes of the melody, beginning with the down beat of m.1. Also, do you recognize the "lick" in mm. 7 & 8 from *Blackberry Blossom* in Lesson 2?

Form: Play Part A twice; then play Part B twice.

NOTES:

1.) In *Katy Hill*, the backup stays on the G chord most of the time, while the melody notes run up and down the scale for the Key of G. Once you have learned this tune, try substituting m.3 from the alternate licks, where the melody note is played on the 5th string.

2.) Part B is for the more advanced player: When 2 notes are played in a row on the same string, the bluegrass style left-hand techniques (H, SL, P) are also effective in the melodic style. It is also fine to pick each of the 2 melody notes using the single-string technique by alternating the right thumb and index fingers. *See the Alternate Part B on the next page.*

Alternate Part B for *Katy Hill* -- for the more advanced Player: (substitute for mm. 17-24.)

Substitute Licks:

75

Lesson 26: *Adding Melodic Licks to a Bluegrass Arrangement*
With Black Mountain Rag

A bluegrass arrangement can use melodic licks and patterns throughout the song or only for a specific chord or passage. *Katy Hill* was played in the melodic style for Part A and in the bluegrass style for most of Part B. The following arrangement for *Black Mountain Rag* is played in a traditional bluegrass style until Part C, the third section.
In Part C, the banjo imitates the fiddle (or flatpicked guitar) by playing melodic style licks for the C, G & D chords.
By learning these licks as individual patterns by chord, it will be easy to substitute them in other songs which include the same chords. For example, the chord progression for Part C is exactly the same for the fast part of *Dueling Banjos* and it is like the entire chord sequence for *Bugle Call Rag.* For fun, try these patterns in those songs, too.

Each of the melodic licks below are compared with a bluegrass lick for the same chord for a comparison of the effects.
Play each lick by itself, until you can play it smoothly. Practice looping the measure without pausing. Then combine the measures of the melodic licks without pausing. Also, you can combine the bluegrass licks. This is what improvisation is all about.

"C" Melodic LICK FOR THE "C" CHORD (1 measure):
Notice this pattern follows the circular scale, beginning with a note belonging to the "C" chord.
(Do not pause at the bar line when connecting the licks.)

"G"Melodic LICK FOR THE "G" CHORD (1 measure):
To continue the melodic run, this lick is played after the C lick in Part C. (This lick also works for a D chord.)

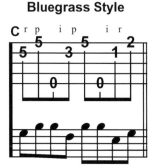
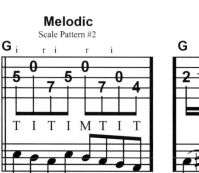
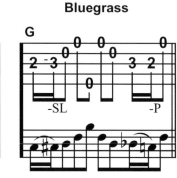

"D" Melodic LICK FOR THE "D" CHORD (2 measures):
Notice this pattern follows the circular scale beginning with a note belonging to the "D" chord.
The second measure is also often used for the G chord.

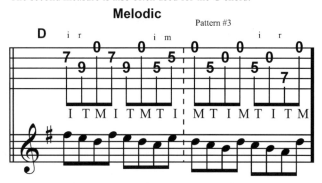
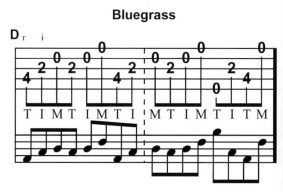

REVIEW: EXERCISE with Circular Scale Line:

At this point, it should be evident that many melodic "licks" which can be applied to specific chords are circular scale patterns which are drawn from the G circular scale. If you practice this scale up and back, these patterns will become very natural and are fun to insert into arrangements for virtually all types or genre of songs.
The scale can begin with any note in the G major scale and be played up or down in pitch. *For more on this scale, see Lessons 9, 10 & 15.*

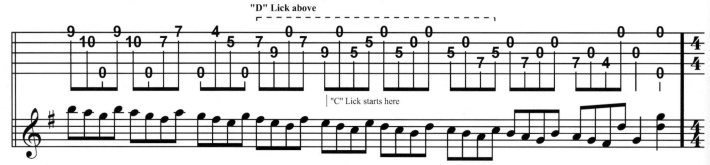

Black Mountain Rag

G Tuning: Key of G
Capo 2nd Fret for Key of A

TRACK 45 Slow

Track 46: Fast
Track 50: Key of A Fast

Black Mountain Rag is well known among flatpicking guitar players, although it was composed by a fiddler. Doc Watson's version for the guitar has influenced many professional banjo players to play Part C in the melodic style. This tune is divided into three parts. It is often easiest to learn by working on one section at a time. Section A and Section B are played in the traditional 3-finger bluegrass style. Section C includes the melodic patterns presented on the previous page. An alternate Section C is also included at the end, for comparison between the bluegrass patterns and the melodic style patterns. These are interchangeable.

Alternate Part C: Bluegrass Style

Substitute Lick for Part C::

Uses Rhythm Pattern also common in the Melodic Style
-- see *Whiskey Before Breakfast.*

Tag Ending: Optional (Add to end of Part C, after m.32.)

TRACK 48

TRACK 49

TRACK 50 **Key of A Fast**

G Tuning
Key of G

Lesson 27: Playing A Bluegrass Song in the Melodic Style
Creating Melodic Arrangements for Bluegrass Songs
With Sunnyvale Breakdown

The circular scale comes in handy when playing a bluegrass song in the melodic style, especially if it is a breakdown or song which has melody notes of long durations. When using the bluegrass rolls, the melody note is repeated by the same finger as it naturally occurs in the roll pattern. In the melodic style, playing a section from the circular scale is effective, beginning with a melody note or a note belonging to the chord indicated for that passage. In *Sunnyvale Breakdown*, isolate each pattern according to the indicated chord. The first four measures are played for the G chord. Separate these measures into two 2-measure patterns. Practice each pattern by looping it several times (x5) without making a mistake. Not only will it be easy to play in this arrangement, but the same pattern can be used for the same chord in many other bluegrass songs to create melodic style arrangements. These can also be split into 1-measure patterns. Note: You may notice that the same pattern may work for different chords. The pattern works from the G scale line. Usually, the first note of the pattern will be a melody note of the song and often a chord tone belonging to the indicated chord. If the melody note is a D tone, this pattern may be used for the D chord or for the G chord, as the D tone is common to both chords.

*Keep in mind that each lick is resolved with the first note in the measure which follows it. Dashed bar line means the two are often played together. To hear the resolution, follow each lick below with the open 3rd string.

1. "G" Melodic Lick: G chord 2-measure pattern

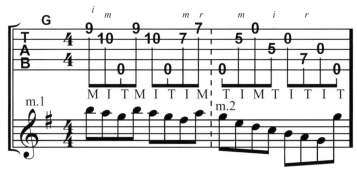

2. "G" Melodic Lick: G chord 2-measure pattern (*or Substitute 1 for next to the last note.)

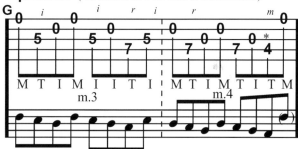

3. & 4. "C" Melodic Licks: C chord
(1 measure) - Interchangeable Licks

Lick from circular scale - last note connects w/G lick
To follow w/bluegrass G lick, substitute open 1st string for last note

Lick from Redwing & Dixie Hoedown

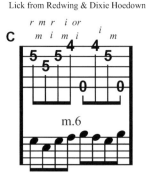

5. & 6. "G" Melodic Lick: G chord (1 measure)
Often interchangeable with the standard bluegrass "G" Lick

Bluegrass G Lick

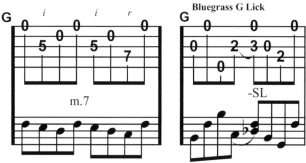

7. "D" Melodic Lick: D chord
(2 measures) - leads to G

Look for the 2-finger L.H. *shapes* in this lick. Hold 2 fingers at a time before picking. Notice R.H. fingering, too.
See the Substitute Licks for more interchangeable D chord licks

8. & 9. "G" Melodic Licks: G chord (1 measure)
Interchangeable Licks

Also interchangeable with the bluegrass "G" Lick (above) Resolves to open 3rd string.

Commonly played after the last D chord, at the end. (This "lick" may also be played for the D chord.)

Fun Up-the-Neck G Lick - follow w/ open 5th string to hear resolution.

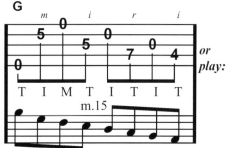

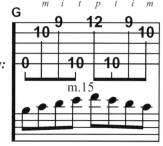

NOTES:____A bluegrass arrangement for this tune can be found in *You Can Teach Yourself Banjo* (Mel Bay Publications).
See the substitute licks to also play this arrangement for *Foggy Mountain Breakdown*.

Sunnyvale Breakdown

G Tuning
Key of G
( ) = optional note
Play or hold previous note.

The following arrangement substitutes melodic scale patterns for the traditional bluegrass licks, according to the chords for the song. These patterns can be used for the corresponding chords in many bluegrass tunes to form melodic style variations.
Look for different occurrences of the same pattern by chord (i.e. for the C chords). Try to find the licks discussed on the previous page with this lesson. Practice these by themselves to make this song easy to play.
Note: **Remember to identify the left hand shapes:** (Shape #1: D7 shape, Shape #2: Barre shape, Shape #3: Partial D shape) as you play through this, and hold both notes down before you pick the strings.

NOTES: _____

1.) *Foggy Mountain Breakdown* uses the same chord progression used for *Sunnyvale Breakdown*, **except the E minor chord is played instead of the C chord for the same measure numbers.** To play this arrangement for *Foggy Mountain Breakdown*, simply substitute an Em chord for the C chord in mm.5-6 and mm.9-10.

TRACK 54

Keep in mind that standard bluegrass licks can also be substituted with chords in this arrangement.

TRACK 55

Lesson 28: Review - Bluegrass & the Melodic Style

A Brief Comparison: These are simple, general comparisions based upon the basic techniques of each style. There are many exceptions and cross overs blending these two 3-finger picking styles.

1.) RIGHT HAND & the MELODY: Both styles use the same fingers: Thumb, Index and Middle fingers. Each finger picks a different string when two notes are played consecutively, unless the preceding note is a longer note value.
Bluegrass: The right hand plays Roll Patterns consisting of 8 eighth notes. The *melody* is usually placed on the 1st, 4th, and 7th notes in the roll pattern so that it is picked by the same finger. (i.e. Forward Roll: TIMTIMTI, Forward Reverse Roll: TIMTMITM, and Backward Roll: MITMITMI.)
Melodic Style: The right hand plays the melody notes along the scale line. Roll patterns may be used, but the right hand usually plays patterns developed from working with the scale. The *melody* notes are drawn from the scale upon which the song is based. Most of the notes played in the melodic style will be melody notes.

2.) LEFT HAND: *Bluegrass:* The left hand usually holds chord positions with the left hand, although when in the open string area this may not be as evident. Bluegrass licks often incorporate left-hand techniques, i.e. slides, pulls offs and hammers. *Melodic Style:* The left hand holds scale positions, usually two notes at a time.

3.) THE 5TH STRING is used as a drone string in bluegrass and as a melody note in the melodic style.

Contrasting Bluegrass & Melodic Licks: The following licks are interchangeable for the G chord in a song.
Play the measure which follows to hear the resolution.

Combining Bluegrass & Melodic Styles: The Bluegrass and Melodic styles may be combined in
many ways. In a single tune, Part A might be played in one style and Part B in the other. Or, the song may be predominantly played in one style, yet also include licks from the other style to add interest, contrast and/or motion.
The examples below form popular 2-measure patterns for the D chord which are interchangeable. These 2-mm. "licks" are often used at the end of a section for the "D" chord to lead to the open "G" chord. For fun and for practice, follow the bluegrass "D" lick below with a melodic "G" lick from the above examples.

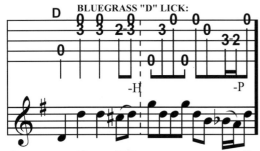
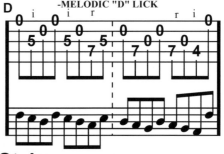

Converting Bluegrass to the Melodic Style: Below, on the left, is an up-the-neck bluegrass
pattern which is converted to a melodic pattern. Try this with other licks by holding the scale shapes instead of the (Em) chord shapes. *Circular Scales* also provide the basis for many melodic style licks and patterns which can be used in bluegrass songs, as demonstrated with *Sunnyvale Breakdown*. Start with a note belonging to the chord. The following is a basic descending circular pattern, which can also be played in reverse, up the scale line. All of the notes are from the G major scale line.
The 1st and 4th notes are the same tone in each four-note group.

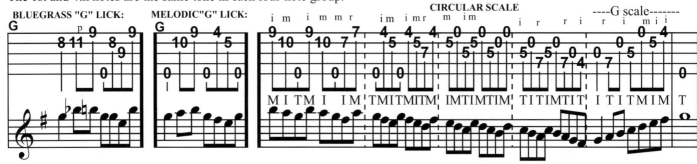

Lesson 29: Playing in the Key of "A"
Without the Capo & Without Retuning

Instead of simply providing a review of the entire book, this lesson will provide the review by demonstrating the melodic style techniques presented throughout the book in an arrangement for *Old Joe Clark,* as it might be played *in the Key of A without a capo.* Compare the following arrangement with *Old Joe Clark* in Lesson 19. This lesson is also intended to provide a preview for how to play any song in any key with the banjo in standard G tuning and without using a capo.

   To move a melody from the Key of G to the Key A without using a capo, and without retuning your banjo, each note is played two frets higher in the Key of A, when the notes are played on the same string(s). In other words, the notes used for the Key of A are played two frets higher than the corresponding notes in the Key of G when played on the same strings. To be able to play a melodic style arrangement smoothly, once you find the notes, move the notes which are difficult or awkward to play, to the *same pitch* on another string in a different location. The same basic left-hand SHAPES apply in both keys. These will help you locate the best positions for these notes. See Lesson 6 for finding the same notes in different locations.

   The following examples demonstrate moving or transposing the first measure of *Old Joe Clark* in Lesson 19 (which is played in the Key of G) to the Key of A. The first step is to move each note up two frets on the same string used for the Key of G. The second step is to play it in the Key of A smoothly. When two notes are awkward to play, move one, the other, or both notes to different strings. They will automatically be played on different fret numbers as well. At first, this may take some experimenting, but keep the left-hand shapes in mind at all times. The Key of A uses the notes in the A major scale, it also uses shapes like the Key of G uses from the G major scale. Note: Each note in the A major scale is played two frets higher from the corresponding note in the G scale, when played on the same string. (See bottom of this page for more explanation.) Note: You can also omit the 2nd note, and play the first note as a quarter note. And, you can change any note that is not an important melody note to a note that is easier to reach (i.e. the 2nd note is a chromatic neighbor tone which could be omitted by holding the 1st note through that beat.) NOTE: ***Old Joe Clark*** uses a G♮ instead of G♯, as it is played in the Mixolydian mode (See Lesson 17.)

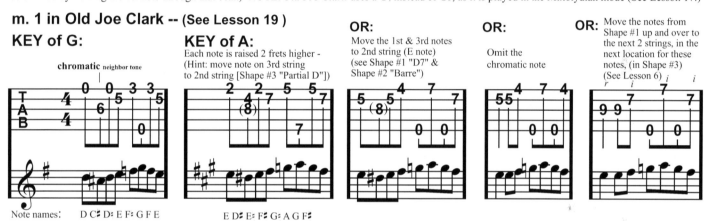

m. 1 in Old Joe Clark -- (See Lesson 19)

KEY of G:

KEY of A: Each note is raised 2 frets higher - (Hint: move note on 3rd string to 2nd string [Shape #3 "Partial D"])

OR: Move the 1st & 3rd notes to 2nd string (E note) (see Shape #1 "D7" & Shape #2 "Barre")

OR: Omit the chromatic note

OR: Move the notes from Shape #1 up and over to the next 2 strings, in the next location for these notes, (in Shape #3) (See Lesson 6)

Note names: D C♯ D♯ E F♯ G F E   E D♯ E♯ F♯ G♯ A G F♯

Note: Each example for the Key of A, above, plays the same notes. Choose the easiest to play. Using the L.H. shapes, if you know where E and F♯ are in each location of the fingerboard, it will be fairly easy to work out an arrangement in the Key of A.

Compare the "G" Major Scale and the "A" Major Scale:

Each major scale uses the same fret distance pattern when the scale is played along only one string.
Locate the first note of the scale, then use the pattern to find the other notes in the scale.
Think of this like a phone number: **+ 2 +2 +1   + 2 +2 +2 +1**

G Major Scale = 7 Notes: The G major Scale uses a fret distance pattern up one string, starting with the note named for the scale (G).

A Major Scale = 7 Notes: The A major Scale uses the same fretboard pattern up one string, starting with the note named for the scale

The G major Scale up one string:

Melodic Style:

The "A" major Scale up one string:

Melodic Style

NOTES:

1.) In the key of A, the melody notes are from the A major scale. Each note in the A scale is played 2 frets higher than the note which corresponds to it in the G scale line. Each back up chord also moves up 2 frets (1 letter name) for the key of A.

2.) To easily transfer a melody from the key of G to the key of A, pick out the melody from G Scale tones on the 3rd string. Then, play each note 2 frets higher to transpose the melody to the Key of A. If you can play the scale in the melodic style, with each adjacent note played on a different string, the left-hand shapes will be a clue for working out a melodic-style arrangement in the new key.

*** 3.) ***Old Joe Clark*** uses a G♮ instead of G♯, as it is played in the Mixolydian mode (See Lesson 17 for the Mixolydian Mode with *Dusty Miller*).

Standard G TUNING
Key of A Mixolydian: NO CAPO
A Mixolydian uses G natural instead of G♯.
(7th note is lowered 1 fret number (1/2 step.)
in the major scale for the mixolydian mode.

Old Joe Clark

TRACK 57 Slow
Track 58: Fast

Compare the following with the arrangement in the Key of G for *Old Joe Clark* in Lesson 19. The same arrangement (set of notes) are now moved (transposed) to the Key of A, using the notes in the A scale. The banjo remains in open G tuning and no capo should be added. Basically, each note is moved up two frets from the Key of G when played on the same string. However, often a note needs to be moved to a different string for easier playability in the Key of A. Once again, the left-hand shapes come into play. If you know where the E - F♯ notes are located in the G scale, then you know where these two notes are located regardless of the key. These two notes are held by the left hand in Shape #1 (the D7 shape) at the 4th & 5th frets on the first two strings and with Shape #3 (partial D shape) at the 7th & 9th frets on the inside strings, as long as the banjo is tuned to standard G tuning. Remember, each new scale alters only one note from the scale which precedes it in the Circle of 5ths.

Form: = Play Part A twice, then play Part B

Substitute Licks

for Old Joe Clark in the Key of A
-- NO Capo --

( ) = optional

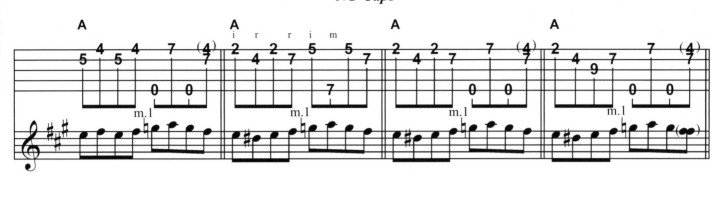

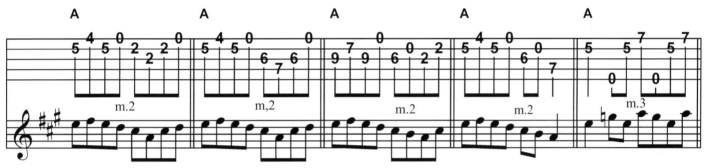

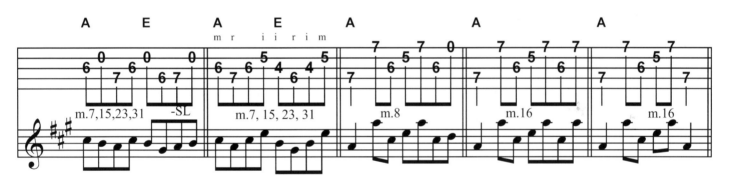

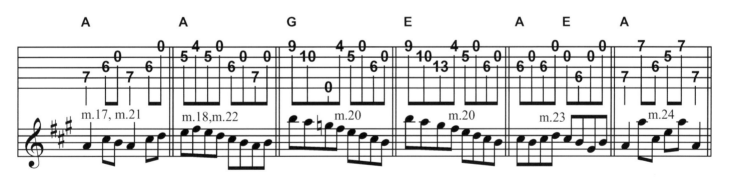

G Tuning
Key of G

Lesson 30: Endings

TRACK 60

When a song is performed as an instrumental without words, a "Tag" Ending is often added *after* the final measure of the song. The "Tag" Ending is usually divided into 2 parts. 1.) A *Signal* that the song is to end. 2.) **The final ending.**
ie. A "Shave and a hair cut " + " Two Bits" The signal = the shave and haircut; the final ending = two bits.
The following examples follow the final measure in the song. Each works for songs in the Key of G.
Play the signal and ending presented left to right, or mix and match each signal with a different ending.
Also, the signal part may be used as a final ending and vice versa in many of these.

Combine the two parts without a hesitation in the rhythm, except as indicated by the notes. There are infinite ways to vary these endings. Also, a pickup note before the ending may be substituted for the last beat in the final measure of the song.

PART 1: SIGNAL: The announcement or warning to the band the song is about to end. Often this will consist of 2 measures.

PART 2: THE END: This, too, may usually consist of 2 measures, (with a final D to G chord.

PICK UP NOTES into the "signal" before the ending add drive and tension:

Substitute pickup notes for the last beat of the last measure of the song (or of the signal as a pick up to the ending section). This is substituted for the open-string pinch.

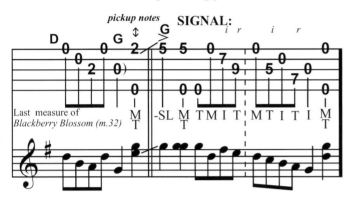

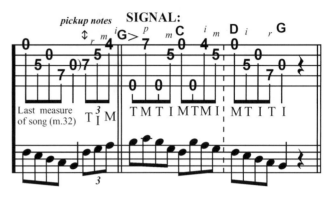

ENDING SECTIONS ONLY: Each example follows any of the above signals as a final ending.

"Two - Measure" ENDINGS:

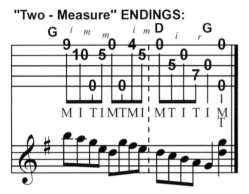

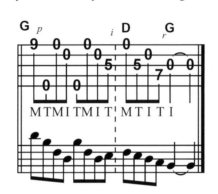

"Four - Measure" ENDINGS: Each of these examples are designed to follow a signal. However, these can also stand alone as a tag ending. In this case, you can kick your foot in the air in order to let the other musicians know the song is ending.

The following 2 + 2 measures = a signal plus an ending, or it can follow a different signal and be played as a 4-measure ending.

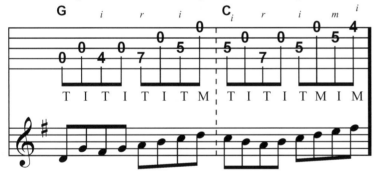

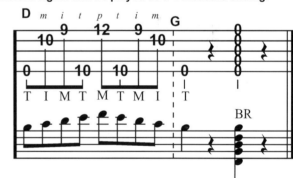

ENDING WITH THE MELODY:

Another effective ending idea is to repeat a passage from the song. The following can be used for *Blackberry Blossom.* Choose the "Signal" from the first examples on the previous page, then play the following as the " Ending":

From measures 5-8 (13-16) of *Blackberry Blossom:*

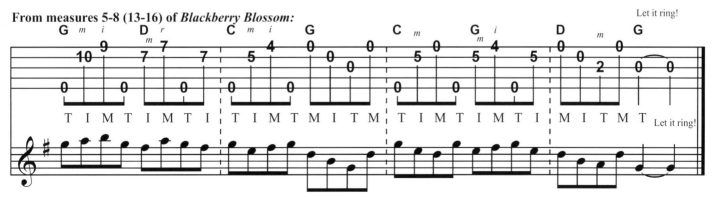

Theme from *Sailor's Hornpipe* for the Signal: 6 measures (signal = 2 measures, mid ending = 2mm.; final ending = 2 mm.)

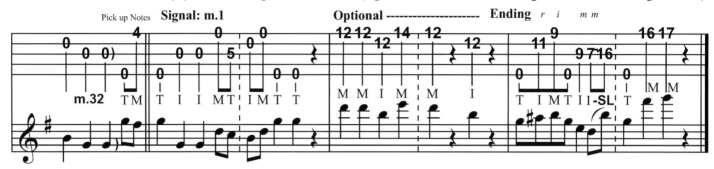

Circular Scale Ending: This can follow virtually any signal as the final tag ending.

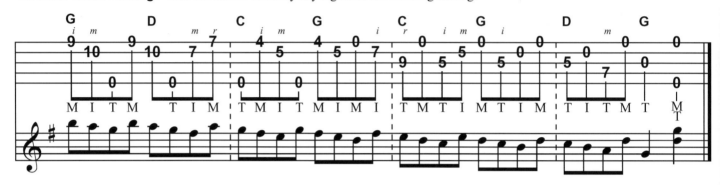

Bluegrass Slides also add motion to the ending. Precede with any signal.

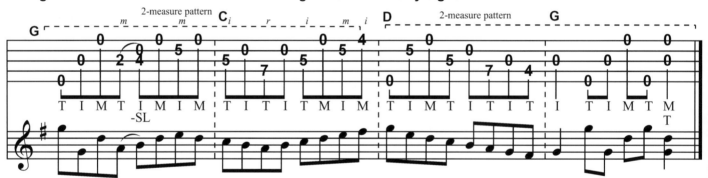

ENDINGS which are substituted for the last G chord of the song.

The following are not tag endings and there is no signal section. Instead, these are substituted for the final G chord immediately after the last D chord. Substitute the following endings for the final two measures (usually mm.31-32) of the song.

i.e. Last 2 measures of
Blackberry Blossom or Redwing

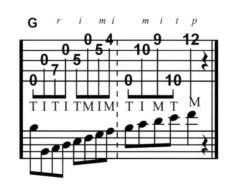
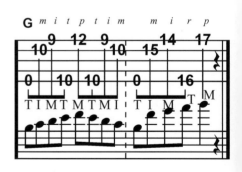

About the Author

Janet Rice Davis was born and raised in Houston, Texas. Music was always an integral part of her family life. Although Janet's formal musical training was primarily in the classical field, she showed a keen, early interest in stringed instruments, particularly those involved in folk and bluegrass music. In college, she performed as a folk and blues musician in many of the Austin, Texas clubs, learning from such greats as Lightnin' Hopkins, Janis Joplin, Jerry Jeff Walker and others who played the same venues. Her instructional books and DVDs for 5-string banjo and Dobro® are popular worldwide. Mel Bay has many of her books and DVDs listed as "Best Sellers." Janet teaches and plays ALL of the bluegrass instruments. She also enjoys teaching and performing at banjo camps and workshops around the country. She has been a regular columnist with *Banjo Newsletter* for over 30 years, and has had numerous articles and arrangements published in other bluegrass magazines. Janet supports the International Bluegrass Music Association (IBMA). Her music company, Janet Davis Music Company-banjo store, specializes in anything banjo & bluegrass.

Other Mel Bay Publications Titles By Janet Davis:

Product Number	Title	Format
93771BCD	**Back-Up Banjo**	Book/2-CD Set
93771DVD	**Back-Up Banjo DVD**	DVD
20285	**Banjo and Chord Reference Wall Chart** (Poster) Chord Chart with note locations on the banjo fingerboard	Wall Chart
94206BCD	**Banjo Handbook** Quick reference: rolls, licks, Scruggs style, melodic, songs, set-up	Book/CD Set
20790	**Banjo Picking Pattern Chart** Chart (Booklet) with almost 200 banjo licks	Chart+Audio Download
97010BCD	**Banjo Scales in Tab** *Recommended companion course with the Melodic Style Learn 1 scale a month – loaded with exercises – play in any key	Book/CD Set
95444BCD	**Christmas Songs for 5-String Banjo** The best of Christmas Carols – O'Holy Night, Ave Maria & more	Book/CD Set
20638	**Dobro® Wall Chart** (Poster) Chord Chart with Note Locations on the Dobro fingerboard	Wall Chart
98530BCD	**Famous Banjo Pickin' Tunes** Star Spangled Banner, I'll Fly Away, Dixie/Yankee Doodle Duet, etc. for all levels.	Book/CD Set
93998BCD	**Splitting the Licks** Improvising and Arranging Songs on the 5-String Banjo step by step with over 30 songs in tab Scruggs Style, Melodic Style, Chromatic Style Beginning-Advanced	Book/CD Set
93998DVD	**Splitting the Licks DVD**	DVD
94820BCD	**Up the Neck** The 5th – 22nd frets of the 5-string banjo – all levels	Book/CD Set
94820DVD	**Up the Neck DVD** with split screen	DVD
94429SET	**You Can Teach Yourself Banjo** Complete course for beginning 3-finger style banjo	Book+CD+DVD
95227SET	**You Can Teach Yourself Dobro®**	Book+CD+DVD

For a current listing of all titles by Janet Davis, call: 1-800-933-5362 (JDMC) or 479-855-0700.

Movable Chord Position Chart
Major Chords

- The number by each individual diagram tells you what fret the chord starts on.
- Use the correct left-hand fingering to form each chord position.
  (I=index; M=middle; R=ring; P=pinky)

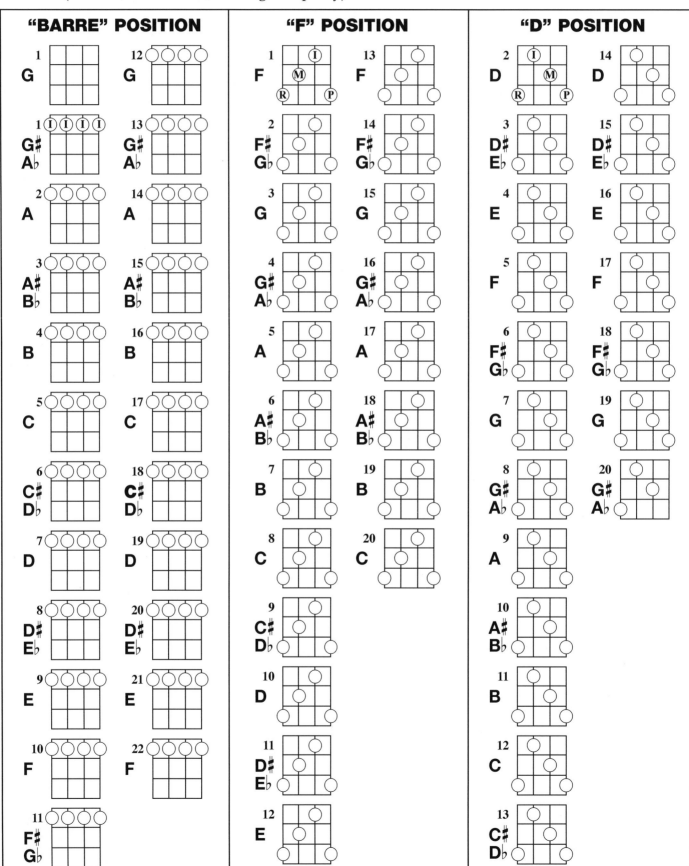

Chord Chart-G Tuning
Major Chords

Major chords are formed from the first, third, and fifth tones of the major scale of the chord name. There are three left-hand positions for all major chords.

The number beside each diagram indicates the fret number where the chord begins.

Major chords provide the primary chords for songs played in major keys. (Most bluegrass songs fall into this category.) In addition, they can also be substituted for other chords in a song, either to fulfill the function of those chords, or to act as a passing chord, or to add color.

Note: ♯ means to "sharp" or raise in pitch one fret. If a ♯ follows the letter name of a chord, the chord should be played one fret higher than the regular position. ♭ means to "flat" or lower in pitch one fret. If a ♭ follows the letter name of a chord, the chord should be played one fret lower than the regular position.

Locating Chords Without a Chart

    • Notice on page 90 that the chord names change in alphabetical order as each chord position pattern is moved up the fingerboard. (The musical alphabet = A through G, repeated over and over.) Notice that B is located next to C and also that E is next to F, but that all other letters are separated by a fret. (The frets in between work like the black keys on a piano.) To locate a specific chord without a chord chart you can start with one of the chord position patterns, such as the "F" Position F chord, and move it up the fingerboard until you arrive at the desired chord alphabetically. If you know all of the positions for the G, C, and D chords, you can also find the other chords in relation to these chords. For example, the E chord is always located two frets higher (in pitch) than the D chord.

    • ♯ means to "sharp" or raise (in pitch) one fret. Therefore, any chord with this symbol following the letter will be located one fret above the position of the chord letter. i.e. G♯ is located one fret position above the G chord.

    • ♭ means to "flat" or lower (in pitch) one fret. Therefore, any chord with this symbol following the letter will be located one fret lower than the regular position for this chord. i.e. B♭ is located one fret lower (in pitch) than B.

    • Minor chords, diminished chords and augmented chords can be located by first locating the normal major chord position of the desired chord. Each of these chords requires altering a tone of the major chord. (See chart for more explanation.) The following diagrams demonstrate how these chords can be located from the major chord positions.

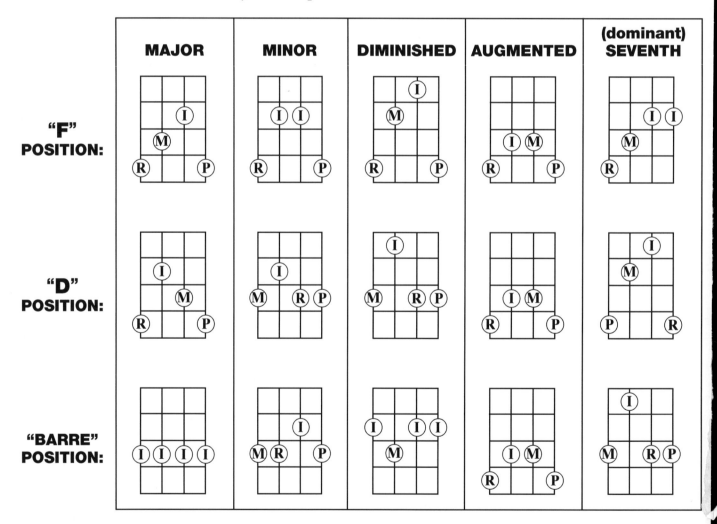

NOTE: Barre the left index finger across the strings, when it is indicated on more than one string in a chord position.

    • A number following a chord symbol (i.e. G7=dominant 7th chord) means that an extra tone is added to the chord. (The major chord can also be substituted for chords of this nature.)

CD #1 Index *(61 tracks)*
Introduction through Lesson 14

CD #2 Index *(60 tracks)*
Lesson 15 through Lesson 30